Mental Exercise For Dogs

No More Boredom! Stimulate Your Dog's Brain
Development and Strengthen Your Bond with
The Best Agility and Intelligence Exercises,
Without Sacrificing the Fun!

Bear Carter

About the author

Bear Carter was born in North Carolina in 1982. He is a famous pet specialist and vet in the USA. He was graduated from the Ohio State University in Doctor of Veterinary Medicine (DVM). He had a plenty of experiences on handling cats and dogs. This book is part of his working experience.

Table of Contents

Introduction

Taking a comprehensive approach to your pet's health and wellness is necessary for ethical pet ownership. The health and happiness of your dog are significantly influenced by training and exercise. Their time with you is probably their favorite time of the day, so spending time with them as they learn new skills, play outdoors, or engage in physical activity together fortifies your relationship.

What kind of exercise does my dog require? How much should I train my dog? Can my dog amuse themselves? Since each dog is unique, finding the appropriate mental and physical activity for them will require customization. Finding activities that match their interests and degree of activity is enjoyable. We have some ideas for both physical and mental training to aid you in your mission.

We all agree that a dog's health depends on having adequate physical activity, but mental exercise is less often stressed. Dogs are very intelligent and inquisitive, and humans often underestimate their abilities. As a result, dog owners should spend time doing activities with their dogs that promote mental abilities like focus, memory, and problem-solving.

There is some evidence that exposing dogs to mental games improves their disposition, attitude, and sleep routine. If you want your dog to be exhausted and sleep well at night, you might try intellectually stimulating them throughout the day. Our animal friends may become tired much as we do after a long day of work or school, or after a week of learning something new. There has been a lot of research on the canine brain. Research shows that dogs are far more perceptive than people give them credit for. Canines may learn to count to twenty and understand concepts like object permanence, in addition to reading human facial expressions.

When dogs are bored, they may resort to behavior that their owners would consider undesirable. People may mistake your dog's attempts at self-entertainment for negative behavior or destructiveness. For these reasons, it's essential to provide mental stimulation for your dog on a daily basis. Giving your dog lots of opportunity to investigate and explore when out for walks may be a simple way to provide them mental stimulation. You may play many other dogs brain games, however, if you want to go a step further.

Chapter 1

Dog-Friendly Instruction

The sheer quantity and scope of contradictory training advice might be perplexing when it comes to dogs. In fact, there are a number of various dog books that are available in bookshops and animal-related stores, and each one offers a different training strategy. Some books say to jerk the leash, while others say not to jerk the leash; some say to use food, while others say not to use food; and still more say to always do this or never do that. Worse still, for many years, a large percentage of humans have connected dog training with harsh techniques such as leash jerks and choke collars, leading them to believe that the process as a whole is laborious and challenging.

False, false, false! In the world of dog training, an amazing revelation has been made: teaching your dog is enjoyable! Even better, training gets quicker and more successful the more fun you and your dog are having. The continuous increase in popularity of reward-based training during the 1980s and 1990s spurred a revolution that was dog-friendly, which is fortunate for current dogs. This transformation began in the 1980s.

Concentrating On Rewarding Positive Behavior

The training of your dog should work toward accomplishing two different goals: the main aim and the secondary goal. The primary objective of kind and smart pet dog training is to inculcate in dogs the behaviors that humans want from them. Teaching dogs not to engage in behaviors that we don't want them to is a secondary objective and one that is considered less vital. The primary objective of teaching your dog to be friendly to other dogs is to show him how to behave in a way that will earn him treats. This is the most straightforward approach to teaching your dog.

You don't really have that many things to teach companion dogs since there aren't that many behaviors that humans would consider to be "right" for them.

The problem is that there are an unlimited number of "wrong" things that pets may do, so it would be exhausting and unpleasant to try to train your dog by disciplining him for every mistake. Your dog won't have the time or motivation to act badly after you've trained him to constantly concentrate on positive behaviors and dependably comprehend you. There are many unsuitable options and often just a handful of acceptable ones for each natural canine behavior you can think of. Consider how wonderful and simple it would be to take your dog to that location whenever he has to relieve himself and to reward him for doing so. This site might be either outdoors or indoors, on paper or pads.

Teaching the right way is simpler than teaching the wrong way.

The cornerstone of training dogs is rewarding excellent behavior. The most crucial choice you will make in terms of training your dog is whether to emphasize incentives or penalties. It is not only simpler to accomplish this, but it is also more enjoyable for both you and your dog. Since there are so few appropriate behaviors, there are a seemingly limitless number of inappropriate ones.

- "Right" Actions
- Eliminating where appropriate
- Interacting civilly with others
- Playing pleasantly with canine companions
- Using dog toys for play
- Taking care of your demands
- Quietly snoozing inside
- Greeting others when seated
- Taking a leash gently
- "Wrong" Behaviors
- Removing from the home
- Rough-housing with others

- Picking at your clothing
- Chewing on your household items
- Savoring your plants
- Eating your shoes
- Using your toys as gum
- Following the cat
- Sifting through your garden
- Consuming food that is not on the table
- Disputes between dogs
- Protecting items
- Bouncing up on guests
- Refusing to comply with your wishes
- Pulling on the leash, rifling in the trash
- Eluding me
- Long-lasting barking

Imagine the time and effort required to correct your dog for each of the hundreds of inappropriate locations where he may have discharged himself. Imagine your home after your dog has chewed on every inappropriate item it can find. If only you had trained him to just use one certain area for bathroom breaks or hooked him on a chew toy, things would be so much simpler now.

Capture Your Dog's Good Behavior!

Maybe it's just our inclination to overlook or downplay acts of kindness in favor of scrutinizing those that violate our values. At least five times a day, you should be able to catch your dog doing well and thank him for it. As time goes on, your dog will get better at figuring out how to grab your attention, making this process much simpler for you. If he comes up to you and sits down in front of you as a kind gesture, tell him how much you appreciate his thoughtfulness. The more often he displays appropriate conduct, the less opportunity he will have to engage in undesirable activities.

The importance of praising excellent behavior extends well beyond that. For the obvious reason that once you've taught your dog proper behavior, he'll stop acting badly on his own. And when he behaves himself, you have no grounds for reprimanding him. Do yourself and your dog a favor and start training him from the moment he enters your house. Get a dog now if you don't already have one. When puppies are young, it is very important to instill in them the value of doing what is right. The minimum age for enrolling a dog in obedience lessons was six months only a few short years ago. It's the same as if we didn't send them to school until they were in high school! Most of those untrained dogs were severely out of control by the time they were 6 months old and needed training techniques that were both physically and emotionally demanding.

Thankfully, we no longer live in that era. Trainers, veterinarians, those who work in animal shelters, and breeders are all in agreement when they say that new dog owners should begin training their puppies as soon as they bring them home. Avoiding pleasure and protecting against future difficulties Trainers who are sympathetic to the needs of dogs put an emphasis on eliminating problematic behaviors via control and the avoidance of reward. If you don't allow your dog off leash while greeting people at the front door as a kind of preventive management and no one ever rewards him for leaping as a form of lack of reinforcement, he won't get much experience at it, he won't like it, and he will instead attempt to figure out what you want him to do instead of jumping.

If he sits down to gain your attention, praise him for trying something new; this may become his preferred method of greeting in the future. If the undesirable behavior continues, it may be helpful to examine the factors that may be supporting it. Some dogs, it seems, get a kick out of barking, and this is an example of a situation in which the behavior itself is reinforcing. In this case, it's important to give your dog something to do except bark. Why not feed him entirely with food-stuffed toys, keeping him occupied as he works to eat? Or, until he learns that barking too much is unacceptable behavior, you may utilize management techniques like on-leash supervision or restriction to a confined place to prevent him from gaining access to the most interesting areas of your home, such as the entryway and windows.

Preventive Administration

It is without a doubt easier, more effective, and more pleasurable to reward your dog for doing the right thing as opposed to penalizing him for doing the wrong thing. You may also speed up the process by being responsible for your dog's life, which will enhance the possibility that he is accurate. As a consequence of this, a significant percentage of the instruction is transformed into straightforward, error-free learning, and strong correction or discipline is rendered pointless as a result. Straightforward and astute. Until the training takes effect, you should be particularly concerned with management. For instance, you should not allow your dog unsupervised access to your home until he has developed a habit of chewing on toys.

The majority of dog owners provide their pets with unrestricted access to all canine amenities. When dogs do something that their owners don't approve of, they are typically rewarded with treats. For instance, the dog becomes crazy while his dinner is being prepared, and then his owner sets down the bowl. Or the owner keeps walking even when the dog is pulling on the leash. It's far more prudent to take charge of the situation and make good use of these tools in order to train your dog. In both cases, you should wait to start feeding the dog or continuing your walk until the dog is sitting or standing still with all four feet on the ground.

Teaching your dog that good behavior is required to get food, toys, attention, social interaction with other dogs, and outings to the dog park will have far-reaching positive effects. This is the finest method to earn your dog's trust and lead him or her towards a long and fruitful partnership with you.

The value of a scarce resource increases when only a select few have access to it. The law of supply and demand governs the situation. Think about what you could do with $20,000,000! You probably wouldn't jump at the opportunity to earn a dollar by helping someone out. As a result, you should exercise command over your dog's possessions to increase their value. For instance, before giving your dog even one or two of his toys to play with, you should pick up the others and have him come, sit, or lie down.

When he comes to you for a pet, make him accomplish something first. When you serve him dinner, you should ask him to do something before placing his food-filled toy or bowl on the floor. Even better, make it a habit to sit down with him sometimes and hand-feed him a piece of his food; in return for each mouthful, give him a chore to do. This will show him that you value him. Similarly, while walking your dog on a leash, it's important to often pause and wait for him to focus on you by sitting down. His new strategy for making sure the stroll keeps going will be to observe you and sit when you stop.

Give your dog the impression that he can have what he wants from you. The only thing that is required of him is to ask politely, which he may do in this scenario by sitting by your side when you finish strolling. A Dozen Different Approaches to Training Your Dog in a Friendly Manner Learn as you make money. The benefits of teaching your dog that engaging in appropriate behavior is necessary in order to get food, toys, attention, social connection with other dogs, and excursions to the dog park are many and far-reaching. This is the finest method to earn your dog's trust and lead him or her towards a long and fruitful partnership with you.

Attention, Please You may catch your dog's attention by denying him the items he desires. If you want to teach him, he has to pay attention. When your dog listens to you and does what you say, you may let him in on all his favorite treats and activities. You need not feel guilty about bargaining with your dog for a few treats. Dogs thrive when given responsibility. Most dogs kept as pets don't get to do much other than sleep all day. But you have the power to alter that.

If you dog-proof your home so that he cannot reach dangerous locations, you are increasing the likelihood that he will be correct most of the time. If you start early with a new puppy or dog, you may avoid future behavioral issues and the need for punishment. The same holds true for avoiding future issues with your existing dog. Once your dog has shown a firm grasp of the norms of the home, he may be given as much leeway as you see fit.

The "shut the door" concept in dog training refers to restricting your dog's access to dangerous or forbidden locations. Close the kitchen door, keep your dog away from the kitchen, or invest in a trash can with a locking top if your dog has a habit of going into the trash there. If you find that your dog continues to urinate in the bedroom, you should shut the door to the room. It is highly recommended that you limit your dog to a single room, an exercise enclosure, or a crate at all times.

If you keep your dog restricted to one room, he will be unable to engage in any of the thousand destructive behaviors that are prohibited in the other areas of the house. Exactly the same methods are used at home to instill good manners in young children. You wouldn't dream of letting a kid go about alone, would you? You can keep your dog under control while out and about with a few food-stuffed toys and a leash. There are so many issues that might be avoided if this were done that the list would fill a book. Until your dog understands the rules of the home, keeping him on a leash will prevent him from doing things like chewing on furniture or eliminating in the wrong places. This is a normal and expected part of the training process. Once the dog has been trained properly, he or she may enjoy the comforts of home for the rest of its life.

Prepare Your Dog for success

Make it so your dog can't lose by giving him all the advantages. If you do this well, he won't be able to help but act the way you want him to. A dog will quickly learn to prefer chewing on appropriate chew toys rather than other inappropriate household things if you confine it to a cage or a secure room with several food-stuffed chew objects, for example. If he is busy with his chew toys, he won't be able to do any damage to your home or bark nonstop.

Teaching with Mild Discipline

To train your dog to sit, down, or come when called, you must first establish a connection between the Antecedent (a cue, request, or order) and the behavior (the desired action). Teaching begins with the alphabet. Antecedent–Behavior–Consequence The frequency of the behavior increases as a result of the reward (Consequence). For instance, if you reward your dog with a treat every time he sits, he'll soon associate sitting with good things and do it more often.

The dog learns that sitting when asked usually results in a treat by associating the two events via the reinforcement they get. The dog eventually develops a desire to sit when directed to do so. You may teach your dog to sit on command by rewarding him whenever he does so on his own (for example, at traffic lights or when meeting new people). In certain cases, this sit is mandatory. This will teach him that sitting is preferable to standing, regardless of whether or not he is requested to do so. This method of instruction simplifies learning theory, or the science of canine education, to an unacceptable degree. Teaching your dog, the alphabet, however, will result in rapid education.

However, the ability to anticipate or generate the behavior you want to place on cue and increase its frequency is crucial to the art of dog training. How, for instance, can you ensure the dog will comply with your request for him to sit before you give him a treat? The success and efficiency of training largely depend on how you go about it. There are primarily three methods used to foretell or influence actions:

- One is to do nothing and let the behavior unfold naturally (capturing or shaping).
- Using enticing rewards to encourage the desired action
- Third, by providing a physical cue.
- The Meaning of Markers

By using a marker, you can show your dog precisely which action resulted in the reward. Some refer to the marker as an event marker since it happens at the same time as the targeted action. After the marker, the payoff occurs instantly. A sign of approval may be as basic as the word "yes," but it is more powerful when it is accompanied by a clear and audible signal, such as the clicking noise of a clicker. In opposition to your voice, the click sounds the same every time. In addition, your dog will be able to recognize the click far more quickly than you would be able to teach him to recognize a single word (like "yes") out of the many words you are likely to say to him at once.

Your dog will rapidly learn that there is just one meaning to the click: the action I took immediately before hearing the click was sufficient to get a reward. If you and your dog are having trouble communicating, try using this clear, crisp sound. Your dog won't start to establish the connection between the marker and the reward until you've done it many times. To maximize his chances of receiving the reinforcement, your dog will likely repeat the action he took just before you gave him the click. When training with lures and rewards, you and your dog put in about the same amount of work, but when capturing, your dog must perform more of the work in order to get reinforcement. It is your responsibility to keep a close eye on your dog so that you can provide timely and plentiful reinforcements.

This is why almost all working dogs, including bomb detectors, search and rescue dogs, and top competitors in obedience and agility, are taught using positive reinforcement. Dogs trained in this way are known to be well-behaved and happy. Reward training often requires more time up front than lure or reward training does. You have to wait for the dog to do the proper thing before you can begin, and he'll probably make a few attempts until he succeeds. Your dog will make a lot of guesses and missteps during incentive training, but it's vital that they don't get rewarded since it helps your dog rule out potentially harmful behaviors. Your dog will learn what is undesirable the more he makes errors.

Your dog will figure out what you want him to do and will quickly begin to repeat the behavior that gets instant praise. Dogs have a lot of fun with this game. To teach your dog to sit, take a few morsels from his meal, hold them in your hand, and wait for him to sit. Barking and jumping are only two of the many behaviors he could alternate between. Don't pay attention to this and give him a chance to sit down; he will. If he doesn't sit immediately, click or say "yes," reward him with a treat, and try again later. (You may have to take a baby step for your dog to get to his feet.) With continued training, your dog will quickly master the sit position. Your dog will learn to correlate your movement with a sit cue (a click, the word "yes," or any other positive reinforcement) in order to earn a treat. You may now anticipate the moment he will sit by saying the phrase to yourself as you are about to come to a halt after taking a step. This method works well for instructing binary behaviors like sitting and lying down. Rewarding the dog when it does something that isn't quite perfect but is on the correct track is an effective way to shape more complex behaviors like a retrieve or an elaborate trick.

Dogs who have been taught with incentives are motivated to repeat those behaviors. Your dog will behave properly if he knows what you want and wants the treat. If he doesn't, don't see it as a sign of disobedience or spite. Instead, you should wonder whether or not he understands your request in this context and whether or not your rewards are enough.

Dogs of every temperament benefit greatly from reward training, including shy dogs (by boosting their self-assurance) and dominant dogs (by strengthening the bond between them and their owners and producing a dog with a more optimistic attitude). Adolescent dogs are full of energy and excitement; therefore, it is best to educate them through positive reinforcement. It's the quickest way to get a dog to relax. You just pretend the teenager isn't there and hope the dog finally does the right thing. It's the fastest method for teaching a young dog to sit when you stop, stay when you call it, and pay attention when walking on a leash. Dogs learn quickly that silly behaviors like leaping and barking get them nothing, but that being still, sitting, and lying down are like switches that activate your positive reinforcement (i.e., praise, goodies, and play time) system. Anyone, even while sitting back in an easy chair, may engage in incentive training. All trainees, but notably young ones and the elderly, may benefit from using reward-based methods. Punishment-based training approaches are soothing. Positive and thrilling language is unnecessary. You may instead sit back and watch your dog learn. And because you don't issue any initial orders, no one will know what you're up to, so you won't appear foolish if your dog doesn't catch on right away. Don't worry, however; your work will be so obvious that people will stop staring in wonder in no time.

Are Markers and Rewards Here to Stay?

A click or reward is not always necessary once your dog has learned a behavior on command. However, you should keep the signs and behaviors your dog has learned alive and well by reinforcing them with walks, playtime with other dogs, and games of fetch, among other things. If you're teaching a new or "old" behavior in a new setting or with new distractions, however, you'll need to get out the marker and the goodies.

Reward-Based Learning

Reward-Based Learning To persuade your dog to move, you may use the luring technique, in which you hold a treat to his nose and then move your hand into different places. You may educate your dog without physically touching him by using a technique called lure or reward. The best lures are probably items from the dog's regular food, but other options include special treats, tennis balls, and plush chew toys. If you can get your dog to follow the movement of a little bait, you'll have full command over his body. By adjusting the lure, you can teach your dog new tricks, including sitting, lying down, standing up, rolling over, and spinning. Change the dog's pace or where it's headed (come, go).

Concentrate his attention on one thing at a time (chew toys, tennis balls, you). Lure/reward training is an efficient method of getting your dog to like training and the trainer, which is useful for modifying natural canine behaviors such as chewing, digging, and barking. Ask your dog some questions, such as, "Do you like training with me as much as I do with you?" You can train your dog to jump by waving food in front of its nose. He'll nod his head in magical accord. Then, bribe them with the food lure if they agree with you. In addition to its many other advantages, lure and reward training helps your dog learn to feel comfortable among people of various ages and backgrounds.

Anyone who takes the time to ask a dog to come, sit, lay down, and roll over in this kind and rewarding way immediately gains the dog's affection. Your dog will come to like the feel of your hands on his or her body and head. Most importantly, using lure and reward techniques allows kids to earn the dog's respect without having to force him to do anything. Children cannot and should not physically coerce a dog into doing anything, but they can and should use lure or reward training to influence the dog's behavior. Although there are benefits to all forms of reward-based training, lure and reward training stands out as an especially effective and humane option.

Hand-feeding your dog for a few days will help if he shows little interest in the food lure. While you wait, spend time with your dog doing things he enjoys. This might be anything from giving him praise and attention to playing with his favorite ball or toy. Use your hand as bait to get the dog to sit, and then encourage him to join you on the sofa. You may also use a tennis ball as bait, and then love and praise him when he comes. It would be a good idea to teach your dog to exhibit more interest in food using lure or reward training since it is so successful. Leaving your dog's food down for just five to ten minutes at each feeding will teach him to eat quickly and will also excite his interest in eating, so save his meals for training sessions. In this approach, you may train your dog to work for his food at times when he is most attentive to the job at hand.

Mechanical Prompting

For a long time, collars and leashes were essential for training a dog. The mere word of dog training conjured up mental images of a trainer snapping the dog's collar with the leash to persuade him to heel or tugging the line upward and aggressively pushing down on the dog's rump to place him in a sit. The dog seems to respond quickly to physical probing; therefore, it appears to be effective. However, there is more complexity to physical poking than meets the eye, and a qualified instructor is usually necessary to avoid undesirable outcomes.

Many people's methods for teaching their dogs fail because they underrate their own abilities. What comes easily to them after 25 years of practice might be a nightmare for a novice dog owner. The dog may get distracted by the physical touch, and it may overpower any other messages, such as verbal ones, that you were hoping to send. The idea of a hostile response should be given the same amount of consideration. One of Isaac Newton's renowned laws of motion reads, "For every action, there is an equal and opposite reaction." To keep his balance, your dog will likely resist your efforts to push or drag him in one direction by doing the opposite. Many of us won't benefit from jerking around our dogs. The results of physically encouraging a fearful or aggressive dog might be severe. An illustration of this would be tugging on a dog's leash while taking it on a stroll. If done often enough, a dog may associate a painful experience with the arrival of humans or other canines. It's understandable how this may reawaken negative feelings.

Chapter 2

Beginning Exercises

According to an ancient proverb, "A journey of a thousand miles begins with a single step." Your dog will learn these activities as the initial steps on a journey that will last the rest of your lives together. It's crucial to remember that these are only "exercises." You and your dog will develop a common language through these simple activities. The goal is to make these exercises as fun and simple to learn for your dog as possible so that they develop a love of training. No matter how many times you have to practice, how long it takes your dog to master them, or if she executes them flawlessly every time, don't stress about it. She won't, I can tell you with certainty. Practice sessions should be more like play than "commands." Exercises and directives vary greatly from one another. Your dog has to comprehend both the exercise and the idea of "you must" for an instruction to become a command. And this idea won't be covered until much later in the program.

A lot of people assume that if their dog has performed an exercise twenty or thirty times, she should "have it" and perform it reliably every time. Then, when she predictably doesn't, they become frustrated or angry and say things like, "My dog is stubborn" or "She's trying to be alpha over me." She's not, and such reactions can foster an unnecessarily adversarial relationship that's inappropriate at this stage. So have fun, make it easy, and when the time is right, you and your dog will be ready to take training to the next level.

Sit

In dog training, the first step is sitting. It's a simple exercise that not only teaches your dog to sit but also introduces the whole idea of learning. She'll begin to understand that when you engage with her in a particular way—waving a treat around and making sounds—you're looking for a specific response. Once she gets this, she'll learn to pay attention in a more focused way. Before you start, review the sidebars below on timing and treats.

Get your dog's attention with a yummy treat that she really likes. If you're having a hard time keeping her attention, use a better treat. Keep your dog's attention on the treat by holding it close to her nose. DO NOT say, "Sit." Slowly move the treat over your dog's head, and keep bringing it back over her head until she starts tilting backward. Still, DO NOT say, "Sit." Once your dog actually sits, say, "Sit," but ONLY ONCE. Release your treat simultaneously.

What If My Dog Isn't Interested in Treats?

While most dogs get pretty excited over the right treat, for some dogs, treats just aren't a big motivator. So now what? You have several options. First, experiment with not feeding your dog breakfast and then using her kibble throughout the day as training treats. This way, your dog will be significantly hungrier throughout the day and much more receptive to training. If kibble doesn't work, try some higher-value treats. Then, come dinnertime, you can assess how much your dog has eaten during the day and determine an appropriate meal size. An interesting side benefit of this approach is that behaviors learned during a period of deprivation tend to penetrate dogs more deeply and are better retained than behaviors taught in a period of abundance. An alternate approach is to explore different motivators for your dog. For example, some dogs are significantly more motivated by toys and games than by treats. If your dog is one of these, try using a ball as a motivator. See Part 6 for more on this.

Adding Watch

Why teach "watch"? Teaching a dog to watch helps her understand that she should look at you after following an instruction. It's a form of impulse control, and I'm checking in with you. Of course, in the beginning, your dog is watching the treat, not your face. However, in time, this habit can become so well-established that your dog will simply do it any time she has performed something for you.

On the Early Timing of Words and Treats

When you're first introducing a new behavior, it's important NOT to chant the phrase associated with the behavior you're trying to teach. Instead, lure the dog into the position you're looking for—in this instance, to sit—and say the word once as your dog commits to the behavior. Remember, you're trying to teach your dog to associate the word "sit" with the action of sitting. In the beginning, if you chant the phrase over and over, it can make it more difficult for your dog to identify the word with the desired action. However, this is only true at the very beginning of introducing a new concept. Generally, after a dozen or so repetitions, the association becomes established, and you can use the word as a cue to let your dog know what you're looking for.

Down

The next step is introducing it. Often, it's helpful to introduce this exercise on slick floors such as tile, hardwood, or linoleum, as it's sometimes easier for a dog to slide into initially. Once they've understood the basic concept, work on whatever surface you like. Remember, say the word "down" only once and only after your dog moves into the correct position; see the sidebar "On the Early Timing of Words and Treats."

With your dog in a sitting position and her attention on the treat, slowly draw the treat to the ground, luring her to follow. If you lose her attention, either slow down or use a better treat. Be sure to bring the treat straight down. As her elbows touch the ground and she commits to the behavior, say, "Down," but ONLY ONCE. Do not repeat or chant "down." The point is to associate the down position with the sound "down" and the treat.

Down: Under the Leg

If your dog's rear end keeps popping up—which is a common problem for dogs whose legs are shorter than their bodies, such as dachshunds and French bulldogs—try this alternate approach. Some dogs don't actually have to collapse their front legs in order for their nose to reach the ground for the treat, so they'll often just sit sniffing or hoist their rear end. Repeat this sequence five to ten times, and you should be able to dispense with the under-the-leg gimmick.

Sit To Stand

You might ask yourself, "Why bother teaching my dog to stand?" The stand command is a useful exercise in its own right, one whose value you will appreciate later. It's particularly helpful when using the stay command (see Part 5). For now, don't gloss it over. Make sure your dog solidly holds the stand for a moment while you deliver the treat.

Building A Routine

Once you've practiced the first six exercises individually and your dog understands sit, down, and stand as cues (see "On the Early Timing of Words and Treats," page 3), it's time to run them together and create your foundational training routine. In essence, you want to move between all the positions interchangeably and establish a smooth rhythm between any and all combinations.

48

This is the foundation for hand signals (in Part 2), and you should NOT move on to those until your dog can cruise through any configuration of this routine with ease. In addition, you want to start asking for more performances of an ever-increasing number of behaviors before delivering a treat. And you want to vary the order. For instance, in the first sequence shown here, you would go through a sit-down-sit-stand sequence before delivering the treat. Once this is established, practice a stand-down-stand routine, as in the second sequence, and so on.

Hand Signals

Once your dog has mastered the foundational sit-down-stand routine, you're ready to add hand signals. The use of hand signals starts to separate sits, downs, and stands into independent concepts in your dog's mind, and they begin building the bridge from "exercises" to "commands." Hand signals also change the way you use treats in order to begin reducing your reliance on them. The full transition to hand signals involves three stages. Each stage works with the exercises you've learned so far: sit, down, and stand. That makes for a lot of exercises to repeat with only minor variations, and it may seem a bit tedious in the beginning. But trust me, if you systematically follow these routines, you'll have your dog responding to hand signals in no time, and you will have paved the way for genuine "commands." Please don't hurry through these. Make sure you've nailed each stage in all its variations before moving on to the next. Remember, you can't build a solid house on a shaky foundation. If you encounter trouble with hand signals or seem to be moving too fast for your dog, go back to exercise 7, "Building a Routine," until your dog follows you consistently and reliably.

The Three Main Hand Signals

In theory, it doesn't matter what gestures you use for hand signals. The important thing is that each motion is easy for you to do and easy for your dog to understand. Other people and trainers sometimes prefer other gestures, and you can add more hand signals as training continues, but I find these three works best for the three main commands: sit, down, and stand.

A Preliminary Form of Down

You have to teach the down-hand signal in two steps. Initially, do the motion as shown here: With your arm raised, palm out, bend over so you can lower your hand all the way to the ground with the treat.

Why do this preliminary version first?

Because the final version of the down hand signal (which appears next) demands that your dog move away from the treat to get the treat, This makes no sense initially, since every other exercise (except staying, later) asks her to move toward the treat to get the treat. Only when she's nailed this should you move to the final down hand signal.

Down

The final hand signal for down is the opposite of sit. With your hand raised, simply sweep it straight down until your hand is comfortably at your side.

Stand

With your hand somewhere near your dog's nose, pull it away in a line level with her nose and parallel to the ground, with your palm facing her. Remember, if you bring the treat and hand signal above the plane of her nose, she will tend to crane her neck up and sit.

Holding the Treat

As you introduce hand signals to your dog, shift the position of the treat in your hand. Don't hold it between thumb and forefinger, where the visual emphasis is on the treat and much less on the hand. Instead, hold the treat between your forefinger and middle finger, where the visual emphasis is much more on the hand and less on the treat.

Hand Signals Stage 1: 9: Giving the Treat from The Signal Hand

The first stage of introducing hand signals is the simplest: You hold the treat between the fingers of your signal hand, and when your dog performs correctly, you give her that treat as her reward. You should go through all of the routines in this stage in this way before moving on to stage 2. In addition, use your tone of voice and certain phrases that function as "positive and negative markers" (see sidebar below) to convey your level of approval or disapproval and to enhance your communication.

Stand to Sit

Put the treat between your first two fingers and hold your hand flat in front of your dog, getting her attention while you stand. Move your hand up in front of your dog while keeping her attention and simultaneously saying, "Sit." If you've taught her to sit with a treat, she will move back into sitting. "Good sit." Once she's in sit, give her the treat while saying, "Good sit." This functions as a "positive marker" that helps your dog understand when she's done what you've asked for.

Positive and Negative Markers

Positive and negative markers are auditory aids to help your dog understand when she's gotten something right or made a mistake. For instance, if your dog has properly performed a command, your positive marker might be an enthusiastic "good." This is particularly helpful when working with your dog from a distance, since you can't deliver a more physical reward quickly, like a pat or a rub. Some people use clickers for this, but in this book, we're not using clickers, only verbal markers. On the other hand, a negative marker is a phrase uttered in a sharp tone of voice that helps your dog understand when she's made a mistake. The most common is "ah-ah." This is extremely helpful to your dog, especially when you're not near her, to help her understand where the problem is. For more about this, see "On Using Negative Markers". The intelligent combination of positive and negative markers, along with tone of voice, dramatically facilitates learning and profoundly strengthens the communicative and emotional bonds between dogs and their owners.

The Importance of Tone of Voice

Dogs will never understand human language. However, they can easily learn to recognize words, and they definitely understand the tone with which words are uttered. In general, dogs have three tones of voice that they commonly use to communicate with other dogs: high-pitched and upbeat, midrange and level, and low and rumbling. These mean pretty much what you'd think. High-pitched and upbeat sounds are happy and playful. Midrange and level communicate a range of more leveled emotions. Low and rumbling sounds are threatening or angry. Of course, dog communication involves a full spectrum of much more subtle emotions and meaning, and to understand what dogs are expressing, we always have to consider multiple factors, including body posture, social context, and more.

However, for the purposes of training, we can take a page from their communicative repertoire and adapt it to our interactions to improve the quality of our communications. In the context of commands and markers, this means that, for a positive marker, you should use an upbeat, high-pitched tone of voice. For a negative marker, use a low, reprimanding tone of voice. And for general instructions, use an ordinary but commanding tone that is slightly weightier and more attention-getting than your ordinary tone of voice.

Stand to Down

People commonly overlook practicing lying down from a stand since they aren't sure why they'd ever need the dog to lie down from a stand. Don't do that! This exercise leads to a much more advanced and very important exercise called "Down Out of Motion", which is used in both heeling and recalls.

A Note About Clicker Training

Anyone who's perused today's training landscape will have come across "clicker training." Clicker training was originally used in marine mammal training, but in the early 1990s it came into vogue as part of dog training. A clicker is a "secondary reinforce." The primary reinforce is a treat. The secondary reinforce marks the moment that a dog performs a desired behavior with a metallic clicking sound. It builds a bridge to the primary reinforce by marking the appropriate behavior and letting the dog know that a treat is coming. I learned clicker training early in my apprenticeship, when I clicked several hundred dogs. However, I dropped clickers because I found that their "marking and bridging" functions could easily be served with a well-timed "good girl."

Sure, the clicker makes a more precise and distinct sound than a human voice, and it definitely helps people become more conscious of their own timing. But I didn't feel that these advantages outweighed the extra burden on my clients. Most had enough difficulty managing a dog, a leash, and a treat. Freighting them with an extra training tool and a pile of concepts didn't seem worth it. That's why I haven't included the use of clickers in this book. Instead, I emphasize how to effectively use positive and negative markers in conjunction with treats. That's not to say that clickers don't work. They do work. They're just not necessary. This isn't just my opinion. It's also the finding of a study performed at the University of Wisconsin that found that dogs taught without clickers learned their task equally quickly as their clicker-trained counterparts and that the clickers added nothing at all.

In fact, clickers can distract the owner from more direct interactions with their dog. That's because it's easy to get so fixated on the click-treat sequence that one misses a whole host of other cues and signals that would strengthen their connection with their dog and eliminate the need for gimmicks. To be clear, I don't oppose clicker training. Clickers are especially useful for dog enthusiasts competing in any number of dog sports that require precise control at a distance. However, most people aren't "dog enthusiasts" in that sense. They're just everyday people trying to get their dogs trained. Instead of a clicker, just use well-timed praise.

Hand Signals Stage 2: Giving the Treat from The Opposite Hand

Once your dog has mastered the stage 1 hand signals and can move through them as readily as she did when you were luring her around by the nose in the part 1 exercises, you're ready to move on to stage 2 of hand-signal training. In the second stage, you introduce a little sleight-of-hand. You continue holding a treat in your signal hand and use it to lure your dog. However, you also hold a handful of treats in your other hand, which you keep either behind your back or to your side, where it's not so obvious to your dog. You'll continue luring your dog with the treats in the hand-signal hand but start rewarding her with treats from behind your back. Eventually, as you repeat these exercises, your dog will start ignoring the treat in your signal hand—even though it's still functioning as something of a lure—and begin looking for the treat from the opposite hand. That's the bridge to getting rid of the treat in the signal hand altogether, which is stage 3 of hand-signal training.

Hand Signals Stage 3: No Treat in The Signal Hand

You should only move on to stage 3 hand signals once your dog is by and large ignoring the treat in your signal hand, since she now knows that the treat reward will be coming from the opposite, hidden hand. In stage 3, you remove the treat from your signal hand altogether. You still use that hand to give the hand signal while saying the command, but you only deliver the treat with the other hand. At this point, your dog will be cueing on the signal hand and assuming that a treat will be delivered from the other hand. In other words, she will have begun to understand hand signals, and she will understand the words "sit," "down," and "stand" as separate, stand-alone concepts rather than as part of a rote routine (the way they are introduced). One more thing:

In stage 3, start to vary how often and how many treats you give. Still deliver treats fairly frequently, but not every time, and once in a while give a lot (especially if your dog has either given an exceptional performance or had a breakthrough on something she's struggled with), and make these differences unpredictable. Your dog should still expect treats while no longer knowing exactly when and how many she'll get. In behaviorist jargon, this creates a "random schedule of reinforcement", and this should continue for the rest of training.

Random Schedules of Reinforcement

A central component of positive reinforcement-based learning is moving from a steady schedule of reinforcement to a random schedule of reinforcement. In Part 1, you initially use a regular schedule of reinforcement. After each performance of a single command, like sit, your dog is rewarded with a treat. Then you ask your dog to complete a sequence of commands before releasing a treat, which introduces a bit of randomness. Once you start stage 3 hand signals and have successfully removed the treat from the signal hand, adopt a random schedule of reinforcement. That means varying when you deliver a treat and the size of the reward. At this point, don't give a treat after every successful exercise, or only give a treat after several successful performances in a row, and occasionally, such as when your dog hits a new level of performance with a concept she's struggled with, give her a "jackpot": a special, high-quality treat or much more than normal. Interestingly, this will actually increase your dog's motivation significantly, even though she is getting fewer treats for the same work.

This is one of the core insights of "operant conditioning," which behaviorist learning theory brought to the world of dog training in the 1990s. The powerful motivation generated by random schedules of reinforcement has been studied with scientific precision in gambling. If a slot machine always spits out two quarters for every quarter someone puts in, this doubles their money, but eventually this becomes so boring that people will quit despite doubling their money. On the other hand, if a slot machine gives nothing the majority of the time, occasionally returns several quarters, and once in a blue moon reward someone with an avalanche of quarters, the person will sit there all day long (or until they lose all their money).

That's the power of a random schedule of reinforcement. And you can harness that power when training your dog to get steadily improving levels of motivation and performance, even while thinning out the treats. For instance, from now on, ask for three performances before delivering a treat, then five, then just two, and so on. And when your dog does something really well, hit them with a rare avalanche of treats. Throughout the rest of this book, continue to apply these principles to every new training context.

Stand to Down

This exercise introduces a second-hand signal for down—aa large, sweeping motion in which your signal hand starts relatively high over your dog's head, then sweeps down in front of her face and to the ground. This sets up the field hand signal for down—a hand raised straight over your head that your dog can see at a distance. This is very useful when teaching down-stays (see Part 5), emergency stops (see Part 9), and distance downs (see Part 12). It's absolutely key in this exercise that your dog NOT sit on her way to the floor. She should simply drop straight down. If your dog always has to sit before dropping into a down, it will be very difficult for her to learn to do this at a distance out of a full run.

Down To Sit: Adding A Foot Nudge

Some dogs may have trouble popping to a sit from a down position. If that's the case with your dog, add a little nudge from the front of your foot to the front of your dog's foot. That usually does the trick. Remember: Nudge her foot. Do NOT step on her foot. If a nudge doesn't work and your dog still keeps backing up, try placing her with her rear end in a corner so that there's no place for her to back up. And if that approach doesn't work, try "Using the Leash to Demand Sit."

Down Without Bending Over

One hand signal that can hit a bit of a snag is teaching down without bending over to touch or point to the ground (see exercise 8, "The Three Main Hand Signals"). That's because when you just lower your hand to your side to signal down without bending over, you're actually asking your dog to move down and away from the treat, which makes no sense to her at this point. With every other hand signal, your dog follows the treat to get the treat, and she may continue to do that with this hand signal. Here's a technique for correcting that.

The Behind-the-Leg Trick

To overcome this little snag, follow this multistep process. First, practice the "Sit to Down" sequence under "Hand Signals: Stage 1" (page 15) until your dog always hits the ground quickly and is also always looking at the ground, not at your signal hand, for the treat. Remember, this won't work if you give the treat from your hand. Place the treat on the ground for your dog to scoop up on her own.

Once your dog is performing this smoothly, do the same thing, but instead of going all the way to the ground, sweep the treat behind your calf and hide it there. If your dog has come to anticipate the treat on the ground, she'll go all the way down. Once she's down, toss the treat from behind your calf into the area between her feet.

During this exercise, your dog might freeze as if stumped or confused. If this happens, so long as your dog seems to be concentrating, it's extremely important to be still and quiet and not say a thing. Your dog is trying to work out the problem. She is not being stubborn, stupid, or distracted. If you repeat "down" or the environment has a lot of distracting noises, it will break your dog's concentration, and she'll give up. Learn to recognize such moments. Often, after as long as even a full minute, your dog may simply drop to the ground, at which point you must enthusiastically praise her after delivering the treat. Of course, if it becomes apparent that she's given up, is distracted, or starts looking at other things, reboot the exercise and try again.

Adding Distance

In the same way that going from sit to down without bending over can present a short-term challenge, so can going from sit to down if there's any distance between you and your dog. Even though it's exactly the same exercise, for some reason, being two feet away can completely throw a dog off. So we sometimes have to slow down and gradually introduce the notion that "down" still means "down" even though we're five feet away. Also, if your dog has trouble as you increase the distance, cut the increments in half and try again. Take your time with this. Progress might seem halting in the beginning, but your dog will soon figure it out.

On hyper specificity

An Animal in Translation by Temple Grandin is a book I came upon years ago while doing research for another. It's a great book for a variety of reasons. But one thing that got my attention was her description of Australian cattle dogs on working ranches in Australia. These dogs had no problem relating to a man on a horse since they'd seen "horsemen" daily since their first moments alive. However, in many cases, these same dogs needed to be systematically socialized with a man who was not on a horse, even if it was the same man. That's because dogs have a hard time generalizing from specifics to entire categories.

So a man on a horse is one thing and a man not on a horse is another, and Australian cattle dogs needed some extra work to make the connection. That's precisely what I think is going on when dogs get confused about the down command the first time it's given at a distance. Of course, they can be taught that "down" means "down" no matter how far away a person is, but it takes a little extra work.

Stand to Down

Teaching stand-to-down at a distance is essentially the same as teaching sit-to-down. Simply repeat the sequence at ever-increasing distances, and if your dog has trouble with a certain new increment, cut it in half and try again. However, for this exercise, you and your dog need to be familiar with stand-stay. Please don't overlook this exercise, as it sets the stage for emergency stops and distance runs. It's also extremely handy for grooming and examinations.

If Your Dog Moves Forward while Adding Distance

Sometimes, when working on stand-to-down at a distance, your dog will move forward toward you rather than hold a stand-stay. This is natural; she's used to doing downs and receiving treats near you. Here's how to correct this issue: This exercise involves two techniques you haven't used so far: a body block (see "On Body Blocking") and a negative verbal marker (see "Positive and Negative Markers," page 15 and "On Using Negative Markers"). Review these before you begin.

Puppy-Hood Objectives

Have faith in Nature. Your dog has to learn to trust her surroundings. Expose her to new environments, materials, items, people, sounds, and more on a daily basis in a supportive manner. Take her out at least three times a week to keep things interesting.

Personal assurance: Your dog has to learn to trust herself. The better guidance you provide, the more she will achieve. The more she achieves, the more deserving she will be of your admiration. She'll feel better about herself if you give her plenty of credit for things she's done well. Give her at least 10 easy activities to do each day to boost her self-esteem. Have faith in the leadership. In addition to learning how to follow your lead as her main caregiver, your puppy is also forming an opinion about others based on your behavior. The foundation for a lasting bond between you and your dog is laid by your first actions and interactions with it. To win her trust, maintain an upbeat and reliable demeanor.

Receptivity to a Novel Item: Direct her positive energy into exploring and accepting new items. I applaud her for taking your advice. Give her plenty of happy experiences with new things. If you want her to inspect something, touch it, and give her plenty of praise when she does.

Ready to take on new challenges? Make her accomplish a lot of little things so she may accumulate accolades for her efforts. Having her practice new skills under your instruction and get positive feedback can boost her confidence. She'll grow to be unafraid of the unknown as a result, too.

Consensus on the Box and Its Limits: You may help your puppy learn to accept limits on her independence by using the crate and other confinement techniques. If this is not accomplished within the first few months of her life, she will have a hard time learning to accept confinement and limits as she grows.

Solo Flight Training: In addition, your puppy has to become used to spending time on its own. She may gain this self-assurance via crate training for brief periods in a separate room from the family. She will learn that the box is not permanent and that she will not be abandoned if she is let out of it often.

Getting Used to the Appropriate Chewing Devices: Proper chewing manners may be taught with the use of chew toys, redirection strategies, and the availability of acceptable chew items. In Chapter 4, we cover what to look for in quality chew toys.

Getting a handle on the idea of housebreaking Setting up a housebreaking routine will aid in her understanding of when and where to "potty." Setting up a routine with your dog will help him learn when and where to go.

What to Expect from A Puppy?

My ego is the center of the universe. Your dog should live up to your highest expectations. We are essentially their slaves at this point. They are similar to a newborn or toddler in that they have urgent requirements. It's important to remember that this has nothing to do with your puppy being naughty and everything to do with his urgent requirements. Care for them without delay.

Second: Love, love, love. Since this is the infatuation phase, the answer is yes; you will quickly get fond of your new dog. Don't lavish your puppy with too much attention or treats, but do take plenty of photos of him or her. This will be the most challenging element of puppy-rearing, but it's crucial to growing a decent, cooperative dog.

You are in a "holding pattern" of sorts throughout puppyhood, although you may start to develop some basic abilities. Obedience training should wait until your dog is older. Until she is five months old, when she can begin learning obedience skills, it is your responsibility to keep the puppy safe, correct any bad behavior, and introduce new ideas.

Puppies follow their natural impulses. Puppies only have the innate knowledge and responses that come with being a dog. Neither their feelings nor their behavior are within their control. Until we educate them to control their impulses, they will continue to act on pure instinct. Do not reprimand them; instead, refocus their energy and be patient.

Restrictions: Puppies have zero impulse control. They usually act on whatever fleeting thought occurs to them at the time. This is due to some innate drive and some laziness. Don't count on your puppy to be well-behaved all the time or to make excellent decisions. Attempting to "break" your puppy's instinctive tendencies (like mouthing) will not succeed.

By teaching her a new mode of expression, you may help your puppy overcome her natural inclination to chew on anything in sight. Until then, your puppy's faith in you as a leader will suffer from your attempts to apply "quick fixes" to correct these habits. The methods for coping with the biting and mouthing that come with teething are discussed later in this chapter.

Puppies can only "behave," or rather, be kept out of trouble, for short periods of time due to their short attention span. They do get more focused as they mature and learn from us. Know that their attention span is limited, and plan accordingly.

Any effort to correct your dog after its mental battery has drained and recurrent, unsuitable habits have begun will be in vain. Put your dog in its crate so it can relax.

Your puppy can be housebroken, but no matter how much he wants to, his body will not be able to "hold" all of his bodily functions. Your puppy will finally be able to regulate his urinary output when he is around four and a half to five months old. Taking regular bathroom breaks will aid in maintaining this pattern.

Wake Up! Don't get your hopes too high. When our pups are young, we are fully accountable for their care. Puppy behavior is not indicative of adult dog behavior. Recognize her learning barriers and help her overcome them as she moves on.

Chapter 3

Finding Your Dog's Normative Behavior

Here's a breakdown of common canine actions that might help you understand your dog's emotional state. Complete his version of the baseline behavior chart, then have him fill out a copy and hang it up. Every time you see him, mentally go through a checklist.

Known Important Indicators

Detailed instructions on how to take your dog's vitals are included here. Check your results against the graph on the facing page. If you need to contact your vet about a possible concern, have the results of any abnormal tests handy. You may assist the doctor decide how soon he or she needs to visit your dog based on your knowledge of both the current and baseline measurements.

A rectal thermometer is NOT something to be left alone. A broken thermometer, an injured rectum, and maybe some spilled mercury might result if your dog were to sit on or rub his rear end. The temperature reading is complete in under 2 minutes. Keep the thermometer's end in your hand and your dog's continuous company.

First, raise your dog's tail and enter the thermometer into the anus, being careful not to hurt the dog.

Second, while holding your dog up, steady him by laying the heel of your palm on his buttock. This will keep the thermometer in place. If he makes a fuss, such as by clamping or swishing his tail, let it go. When a dog's tail is not restrained, it is easier to take its temperature. A glass thermometer will detect the temperature after approximately 2 minutes, whereas an electronic one will beep after around 30 seconds.

Third, take out the temperature gauge. Glass thermometers need wiping with a tissue before reading. Clean the end with an alcohol swab, and then wash it. Instead, use plenty of soap and water to clean up.

A Stethoscope Guide For Dogs: How To Take Your Dog's Blood Pressure

Get a hold of a stopwatch or digital watch. Do a kneeling squat near your dog's left elbow. Alternately, you may stand to his right and reach over if he is little enough. Gently insert the bell of the scope into his armpit, right behind his elbow. It sounds like his heartbeat consists of a lub and a dub, which should be counted as one. The BPM is calculated by counting the number of heartbeats that occur in 15 seconds and multiplying that number by 4.

Methods for Digitally Assessing Canine Heart Rate

Keep one hand on your dog's collar and the other on the joint between his leg and body by placing your fingers there. Apply pressure on his femoral artery until you feel a pulse. You may also remove the stethoscope and use your fingers to explore the area just above and behind your left elbow. Once the pulse has been located, count how many times it occurs within 15 seconds. The BPM is calculated by multiplying by 4.

Program of Immunizations

Your canine vaccination schedule will likely include vaccinating your dog once per year to three years (or more often, depending on your dog's lifestyle) depending on where you and your dog reside. When should your dog get what shots? Consult the following chart and talk to your vet about whether or not your dog needs the immunizations listed in the right-hand column.

(We've looked in the column for you to see which immunizations are required.) Then schedule the necessary vaccinations and keep to that schedule.

Parasite Control from The Outside

Your dog's mortal enemy is the swarm of bloodsucking insects that plagues him and you. Not only may fleas spread parasites and diseases, but their saliva can also trigger allergies in your dog (such as flea-bite dermatitis). For instance, ticks may spread Lyme illness and Rocky Mountain spotted fever in certain parts of the nation, while fleas can spread tapeworms and bubonic plague.

An Extraordinary Connection

There is nothing else quite like the bond between humans and dogs when it comes to the emotions felt by both species. This relates to our shared evolutionary history and ancient past: During the early stages of human evolution, canines and humans began to interact. The pets we adopted ended up altering us, too. Around 30,000 years ago, when people were hunter-gatherers living in nomadic bands, the foundations for this kind of life were laid. Prior to the development of agriculture, towns, and currency, people had a close relationship with their natural surroundings. Humans have always been good observers of other creatures, what with their carnivorous and predatory diets.

Wolves and these prehistoric people lived side by side, and in certain regions of Europe and Asia, they even had encounters. We were both enticed, although in different ways, despite being of different species. Humans kept wolf cubs in their settlements and camps and even fed them on occasion. While the cuteness of newborn animals across the board is undeniable, there is something irresistible about the fuzzy cheeks of puppies. Today, we humans are much more captivated by dogs than ever before, primarily due to the way canines have evolved as a species over hundreds of years. A wolf pup may be adorable, but an adult wolf is not someone you want to snuggle up to. On the other hand, canines provide a unique set of challenges. Due to centuries of confinement and changing human tastes, dogs now exhibit more "neotenic" characteristics, including those more often associated with children. Dogs, descended from wolves, have bigger, rounder eyes and shorter skulls and snouts.

Some dog breeds, like the bulldog, have been developed to emphasize these characteristics. Mickey Mouse, a character created by Walt Disney, underwent a neoteric transformation by cartoonists, who altered him from his original ratline appearance into a creature with wide, rounded ears and huge, babyish eyes. Some researchers have hypothesized that Homo sapiens underwent a process of "self-domestication" over the course of several million years. As a result, many characteristics associated with childhood or adolescence persist throughout adulthood. In fact, human adults retain many characteristics that other primates only show as infants. We differ from other primates in a number of ways, including the lack of hair, the slimming and vertical development of our faces, and the reduction in the size of our teeth (no protruding canines except for Dracula).

Even as adults, we continue to play (behaviorally speaking; consider all the adult-oriented sports and electronic games). While early canine domestication focused on practical tasks like sled hauling, guarding, and hunting, the value of dogs as friends eventually rose to the forefront. For example, the Aztec and Maya of Central America and the Chinese empire left dogs with social functions ranging from friendliness to status symbols, including burial with novelty objects and portrayals in art, thousands of years ago. Some of the first tiny dog breeds originated in this area; these dogs were too little to pull a cart or hunt bison, but they were perfect as status symbols or tokens of affection.

The Energy Of Cultural Humanity

Several monuments depict the tlalocite, the ancestor of the Chihuahua, which was raised by the Aztec and Maya dynasties. Such dogs never matured physically and always seemed to be young in heart. By selective breeding, the original, bigger "prototype" dog shrank, and a new, more endogenous form was developed by human cultural activities. It's important to remember that dog shows and other such breeding methods aren't actually for the dogs' benefit. Because humans are naturally attracted to neotenous pattern, many modern breeds are aesthetically pleasing. Unfortunately, several of these dog breeds are predisposed to developing chronic health issues. Dogs like terriers and bulldogs have had their body types altered so drastically that they nearly invariably need a caesarean section to give birth to their offspring. Breathing is difficult for other endogenous species.

With Caution Repeated

Insects, like many other organisms, are not immune to the interesting natural pattern known as neoteny. When it comes to popular culture, we humans are suckers for these kinds of repeating motifs, which can be seen everywhere from pets and cartoons to endless online memes. It's amazing to experience a strong kinship with other animals and to really appreciate the unique relationship we have with our dogs. However, we still need to be careful. The draw of neoteric patterns may lead us into certain morally dubious activities, such as the breeding of breeds with lasting health issues, when attraction is fed by human economic practices. Humans, being a neotenic, or "childlike," species, may be especially guilty of engaging in such dubious behavior. But because of our culture and societal structure, we might also reconsider the morality of our present methods.

If we commit ourselves to life with a dog, we want to make sure the animal in question will fit into our lifestyles and our households. Homes with cats or children or those in a busy urban area have different attributes than rural households with lots of space to roam. That's why, when people consider getting a dog for the first time, they often investigate the differences between breeds. When it comes to a dog's overall shape and size, this is a reliable yardstick. We know what we are getting with the appearance of a Great Dane or a terrier. With most pedigrees today, even coat colors are standardized through highly controlled breeding.

But a new study published in the journal Science shows that, as it relates to the realm of behavior, how a given dog reacts to strangers, other dogs, or small children is not predictable by breed. A "friendly" dog is not something you can rely on by choosing a specific breed. It really comes down to happenstance and to parenting, with a large part of the latter being set by the early environment that a responsible breeder can provide. This new study was a large-scale examination of the long-standing question about how individual dogs of specific breeds act and behave. The American Kennel Club, for example, describes particular breeds with keywords such as "intelligent," outgoing," and "affectionate," presumably capturing that group's personality. But we all know that individual dogs behave differently.

And are bulldogs really more aggressive or retrievers more friendly, as the general stereotypes would suggest? The key insight from this study reveals that the answer is no. Those traits vary by individual but are not set at a breed level. The researchers sorted through data from more than 18,000 dogs, provided by their respective humans through a citizen science project called Darwin's Ark. The study also analyzed DNA from some 2,000 of those dogs to probe the degree to which behaviors such as aggression or sociability might be heritable through genetics. Right away, we can note that the sample sizes here are impressive. While many of us know dogs intimately, we do so only in small numbers. But in the careful and slow science propelling the new results, hundreds of different questions that the pooch owners all responded to were examined across a large pool of pups covering over 70 breeds.

This is the main difference between the scientific way of looking at dogs and our everyday way of looking at them: We always live with individual, specific dogs, but scientists study populations and general patterns. The large sample sizes allowed the authors to conduct fine-tuned statistical analysis across a range of behaviors, including whether the dogs in question enjoy getting wet or do circles before pooping. Besides the genetics and the breed, the researchers also accounted for other key categories such as age and sex to locate significant associations. While the sex of the dog doesn't make much of a difference when it comes to the behaviors examined, age does. It turns out that old dogs do indeed learn new tricks.

Threshold Of Anger

When it came to analyzing how easily a dog acts defensively or aggressively toward something unexpected in their environment, breeds made little difference. Or, to put this more precisely, only 9% of the variation in behavior could be explained by breeds. So, when it comes down to living with one or two dogs, a pit bull or a golden retriever are both likely, or unlikely, to act aggressively. Exactly how the chips fall with a particular dog in a particular situation depends on their own past experiences. And the one key feature in those past experiences are the humans in question: those that the dog lives with and who first guided them as a puppy into the world of human social life (with all its arbitrary rules and regulations). But in many ways, the story here reaches back even further: The scientific findings line up with the overall emergence of dogs as a species. The fact that breeds do not make that much of a difference in predicting the overall dog personalities is because breeds.

Across the Ages

The team from Darwin's Ark found another intriguing, if less surprising, pattern among all the breeds of dogs: Across the life span, they like to learn. In scientific approaches to dogs, one of the common variables examined is "bid ability"—how well a dog responds to human attempts to direct them (think of the basics such as "down" and "stay"). As we would expect, the scores in bid ability for older dogs were higher than for the young ones. Indeed, it is difficult to get a puppy to listen to us or, in essence, to understand us as humans (dog moms seem much better at guiding their pups!). This is the more general issue that the broader study rested upon: How well do dogs understand our human communication? After all, for any of us to understand the actual nuances of human communication, it is a long road. For humans and dogs alike, it takes a while to "get" what our fellow humans are up to and what they might be expecting from us. Part of the challenge is that there are many contradictions between our words, tone of voice, and body language. We say one thing, while our actions tell a different story. And dogs, too, have to work with these far-from-perfect processes. The old ideas about the human owner as an "alpha dog" showing dominance have only served to hinder communication, creating confusion on top of everything else. So, before we get upset by the fact that our dog doesn't follow directions or end up blaming their breed, we might take a pause to look at how consistent we ourselves are in what we are trying to communicate. As with all learning, small steps in training make for good progress, especially when both the human and the dog are adapting to each other. This is what we have been doing as a species for tens of thousands of years. The biological potential for us and dogs to work together, to live together, and to cooperate is there. A wolf cub won't work in this setup, but any dog pup has this potential. As many dog trainers like to say, let's do our part to "set them up for success. Dog training is quite new, relatively speaking, with most having been created in the late 1800s. Indeed, the breeding practices that we are now familiar with only emerged in Victorian-era England, when people began to associate social status and prestige with "purebred" dogs. This was all part of the enthusiasm we humans have for controlling nature to ever greater extents.

A Species Apart

The real change occurred when dogs evolved from wolves—earlier in the evolution of canine species. This is the big difference, and the one that will predict whether a pup has the potential for life in human society or not. While dogs and wolves today share some 99.96% of their genetics the two species are distinct. With proper guidance and a little bit of training, any dog puppy can learn to live with humans, whether in urban or rural places. Indeed, dogs as a species are biologically sculpted for this shared life journey with humans across cultures. But wolves are not. It doesn't matter if you raise a wolf cub by hand before their eyes are even open (thousands have done this); you simply will not end up with a canid that can go to the park with you. This is the case because of the degree to which humans have been interacting with the lineage of candies that dogs come from for over 30,000 years or even longer. Ancient bones from Europe and Siberia tell a clear story of change over time. In comparison to wolf remains from the same era, the skulls of these early dogs are shorter, the teeth more crowded and the bodies smaller. Gradually, over time, their actions changed too, and today's dogs are, first and foremost, still dogs more than representatives of any given breed. What the current study shows is that the dog's fundamental nature is shared across breeds and all those happy, sweet mixtures we call "mutts."

Like Owner, Like Pup

My late cockapoo Connor used to react blatantly to my moods, voice, and facial expressions. I was aware of this and played with it. Whenever I was about to take him out, I'd approach the door and blurt excitedly, "We're going for a walky walk!" and he'd hurtle off the couch or floor and tear full speed to the door. At other times, I'd put on a song and happily dance around the room, and he'd kind of dance along with me, but really put his legs up on me to stop and reclaim me, nonplussed by this sudden, wild, inexplicable activity. Yet other times I would forget myself around him and get angry at someone or at the world, swearing loudly or just looking frighteningly enraged, and this would so unnerve him that he'd run to my wife in another room for shelter and succor.

You Are Your Dog's model.

I regret those moments, especially now that research is showing how seriously dogs may be affected by and reflect their owners' attitudes and actions. For example, in a 2021 study out of the School of Veterinary Medicine at the University of Pennsylvania ("Penn Vet"), the investigators found that for dogs with behavior problems that were enrolled in an intervention program, their owners' personalities and their level of attachment to their owners played a significant role in whether they improved or failed to improve their behavior. According to Stanley Coren, PhD, professor emeritus of psychology at the University of British Columbia and an expert in animal behavior, "this study observed the effect of owner personality on dog behavior." The bottom line is that dogs react to their surroundings, which are mostly controlled by their owner.

A standardized behavioral assessment instrument called the C-BARQ (Canine Behavioral Assessment and Research Questionnaire) was used to examine each dog. Researchers also measured the owners' "Big 5" personality traits, the most fundamental aspects of a person's character: extroversion (whether the person is outgoing and sociable versus solitary and introverted), agreeableness (whether the person is warm, cooperative, and considerate), conscientiousness (whether the person is organized, reliable, and emotionally stable), and neuroticism (whether the person is emotionally unstable or not). Penn Vet animal behaviorist and C-BARQ developer James

Serpell, PhD, says that one of the most important discoveries involves the owner's receptivity to new information and experiences. Dogs whose owners exhibited this characteristic—"openness to new ideas, lack of conservatism"—showed substantial progress over time, as noted by Serpell. "That makes sense, since people who are open to new ideas would respond positively and have a positive effect on the animal if they went to a veterinary behaviorist who told them the possible source of their dogs' problems and gave them new ideas about how to handle those problems." "Really, the key dimension of openness is intelligence, with some creativity stuck in," argues Coren. People who are intelligent are curious, open to learning and new experiences, and receptive to other points of view. They have the greatest opportunity to mold their dog's behavior for the better.

Aim For Optimal movement.

A lot of dogs are literally held captive in the home. They get one walk around the block twice a day, but they're never allowed to move their bodies and build their muscle tone, get rid of all that nervous energy, decrease cortisol (a stress hormone), or lower their blood sugar. And that leads to both physical and behavioral complications, according to veterinarian Karen Becker, DVM, co-author of The Forever Dog. Becker notes a correlation between the longest-lived dogs in the world and the amount of exercise they had—at least an hour and a half a day.

Encourage Foraging

Many trainers say that you should try to feed your pet with a food puzzle—a toy that makes the pup work to release food—as often as possible, even daily. Idealists among them believe that, especially for working dogs and other very intelligent breeds,

100

the bulk of their eating should be through food puzzles, so they can in a sense earn their keep like they traditionally have through the millennia. Food puzzles can be fun and build confidence, plus they may stop your pet from overeating by wolfing everything down.

Detox Your Dog

"Sometimes our dogs are in such toxic environments that no matter how clean you are as a human, you are unable to scrub their Dogs need some unrestricted exercise for muscle tone and aerobic and heart health. Bloodstream of all the chemicals they're carrying," Becker says. But "there are supplements that can pull those toxins out of the bloodstream. There are foods that can specifically detox cancer-causing toxins in dogs." If you live in a highly polluted environment, you need to get a good air purifier that removes particulates. If you've got black mold, you need an air filter. If you live in an area with a known water contaminant, filter your dog's drinking water (and your own!).

Watch Out for Damaging odors.

As a corollary, do not surround your dog with overwhelming scents or wash away natural smells. Do not wash your pup with sanitizing shampoos or douse them with perfumes and scented lotions. For a creature whose identity is so firmly rooted in scent, this could cause them to lose their sense of self. While you should generally keep your home free of invasive smells, one study found four scents that can relax your dog: vanilla, coconut, valerian, and ginger.

Eliminate Stress

We all know that stress can literally make humans ill, but your inner anxiety can sicken your dog, too. Remember, your dog can smell the stress hormone, cortisol, that your anxiety has produced. "They can analyze your entire day," says Rodney Habib, co-author with Becker of The Forever Dog.

"You could have fought with somebody in the morning and been over it in the afternoon. Yet when you come home in the evening, your dog can smell that fight." The second your dog smells your stress, according to researchers, they become that stress. Instantly, their own cortisol levels go up. So if you can do nothing else for your dog, keep yourself balanced and reduce the stress of life through exercise, yoga, and even cooking.

Dreamland of your pet

The members of the study team implanted electrodes into the rats' brains and then recorded the patterns of brain activity that happened in the hippocampus while the animals were awake. The hippocampus is the region of the brain that is responsible for storing knowledge about our experiences. Wilson makes the observation that "it's sort of like recording a movie of the experience." After that, when the mice went to sleep, the researchers watched their brain activity to determine whether the patterns recurred while the animals were sleeping. Wilson adds that it is possible to record in parts of the brain such as the visual cortex and see patterns that match what the subject sees. "And what we discover is that those patterns repeat even while we are sleeping. We see the same patterns, and we see the patterns in the same sequence, as if the animal were moving through the environment and seeing the visuals that were linked with that.

That's as close as we can get to identifying what animals might be experiencing during sleep—what we would call dreams. So we can say the animals experience these things as well." Wilson thinks it's fascinating that animals, particularly mammals like rats and dogs, share the same pattern of sleep as people do. In particular, Wilson is fascinated by the fact that animals dream. There are two distinct phases that may be distinguished from one another: rapid eye movement (REM) sleep and non-rapid eye movement sleep. People who have been awakened from REM sleep report experiencing dreams; this stage of sleep is sometimes referred to as paradoxical sleep since brain activity during this stage seems to be similar to that of an awake brain. Researchers led by Wilson and his colleagues discovered that the brain activity of rats during REM sleep related to the experiences the rats had, such as finding their way through a labyrinth.

"It's as though the animal is actually running or actually moving through space, having these experiences," he says. "That relates to what people might think of when they're watching their dog. Your dog's asleep, and you suddenly see these periods where their paws might start to move, and you hear their half-vocalizations. And you think, 'Oh! They must be dreaming about chasing squirrels or running around.' That would be these periods of REM sleep, where the dream content also includes movement." According to Wilson, there are more substantial reasons than simply curiosity to care about why and how dogs and other animals, including people, dream. First of all, several studies indicate that the brain employs memory processing when sleeping or dreaming to carry out crucial processes and make sense of the environment.

He explains that as we sleep, our brains work to "make sense of complicated things." This has a significant impact on the social lives of dogs. We can use a word and a hand gesture, then a clicker or a "yes!" and a treat or praise to teach a dog to "sit" or "come" when called. But dreaming aids learning beyond just memorization by allowing us to consider the nature of the connection we want to establish with them. Teaching them not to jump on you or your friends or to race ahead of you as you walk is part of your mission as their human companion. That's the big mystery," he explains. And I believe sleep has a special contribution there. Providing our dogs with enough time to rest is an important step in training them to think strategically. Animals, as we have shown in our studies, have aspirations and find value in education. As Wilson points out, "selective interference with effective learning" is possible via manipulation of sleep and dreaming.

Impact of Sound

Sleep-related sound stimulation has also been established in experiments. Both humans and dogs go through the same sleep cycles, including the rapid eye movement stage that indicates dreaming. For humans, the fact that our environments may shape our dreams is hardly a revelation. "If you're cold, you might dream about escaping on an iceberg or something like that," Wilson explains. And similar data may be recorded when rats sleep. We can observe that a person's dreams may be triggered to repeat information related to something they heard while awake by playing noises linked to that something.

Dogs are likely mimicking this behavior, at least in part. Their dreams are probably being influenced by the things they hear. According to Wilson, the auditory cortex (the region of the brain that processes sound) is just as active during sleep as it is when awake, making sounds a particularly potent environmental influence on sleep and dreaming. Even if a dog doesn't seem to pay attention to what's being said to him, his brain is still absorbing the information. In theory, you might direct their actions while they sleep and alter the way their minds work. He replies, "I imagine if you told them to sit in their dreams, they would. However, Wilson warns that this constant listening for potentially significant noises, like a warning from predators, might have negative consequences.

This means that the dog might be disturbed by unexpected noises; optimal sleeping conditions include complete darkness and minimum stimulation. " Here's how I feel about it: Evolution wisely made sleep serve its purpose. If that's how it's supposed to function, then I'll leave it alone. He claims that a good night's sleep is directly linked to optimal mental wellness. " It may have metabolic benefits. It's crucial for not just processing memories but also maintaining a healthy brain and body. Therefore, I would not recommend that anyone wake their pets when they are sleeping.

5 Ways to Protect Your Dog

Use Booties

Dog shoes are sometimes seen as frivolous fashion statements because, as myth has it, a dog's feet are immune to the impact of cold, ice, or scorching heat. But booties also happen to protect our beloved canines from frostbite and salt or other chemical deicers on winter streets and the burning hot pavement in the summer months.

Teach Your Dog Human Language As Early As Possible, Preferably When He Is A puppy.

It's not just about communicating with you. Teaching some basic human vocabulary (using gentle training techniques and delicious rewards) will keep your dog safe. Start with his name (the more you use it, the more likely your pup will know you are referring to him) and the most basic of all commands: "Sit." Then, most important, are the words that allow your dog to explore safely because, when it is time to stop, he will know to desist and return to you: stay, stop, come, and down.

Dog proof Your Home Just Like You Would Childproof

IT Only leave out things your dog is allowed to play with. Dogs are not humans, though they live in our A dog who can follow your directions will be safer when a risky or unexpected situation pops up. homes. We must make it easier to live in our environment and play by our rules. And don't punish your pooch if he tries to play with something off-limits, such as a TV remote. Simply redirect her to a toy that she is allowed to chew and play with.

If You Have a Dog Family, Scout The Group For bullies.

If you have a family of pets and suspect one of them may be bullied, do a consent test: Separate the two animals, then let the dog that seemed to be the victim go. If he runs back to the other side to keep on playing, that tells you it was just fine. If not, then keep those puppies separated and find a way to keep your older dog safe by giving him a "room" or space of his own.

Avoid The Hidden hazards of sticks

Be careful if your dog runs or swims with a stick in her mouth. Experts say that this seemingly innocuous activity can end in terrible tragedy. Veterinarians report a steady flow of dogs who have accidentally impaled themselves with sticks. "As soon as you say the trigger word—stick—the first place I'm looking is the mouth and the back of the throat. Unfortunately, sometimes it takes sedation to see far enough back into the throat where the injury is," Alaskan veterinarian Paige Wallace, DVM, writes in her blog. Stick injuries prevent dogs from eating and may become badly infected as well. To avoid this problem, Wallace suggests supplying your yard and car with toys your dog can play with easily. That way, it will be easier to resist the urge to toss a stick at your dog.

Chapter 4

Your Dog Has Emotional requirements.

Your dog has a high capacity for learning despite her current modest mental requirements. Her desire for sleep is far greater than her demand for cerebral stimulation. The lessons she is picking up through her investigation and the way the world reacts to them, however, are invaluable. She requires reinforcement for her efforts to learn, both from you and her surroundings.

Think of all the time you spend with your puppy as a chance to educate it. To be effective, these meetings must be upbeat and well-guided. Her propensity to misbehave increases if she is not properly monitored or if her supervision falls into the "half-supervised" category. Making the same errors over and over and having to keep being told off is not a good time for anybody.

The "lessons" you give your puppy should be brief. Puppy dog training is hard work! They are attempting to adapt to human society, which means that their natural "doggie skills" (such as rough play, food guarding, mouthing, etc.) don't work. Both his learning and "unlearning" need to be done in small increments.

To prevent mental fatigue and frustration, crate your puppy at regular intervals throughout training. A puppy that is overworked or unhappy is not going to take to training very well. She'll be ready to go again after some rest in her crate.

Exploration at this age is often motivated by curiosity rather than innate drives (such as hunting impulses), so it is less likely to result in recurring nuisance behavior. An "ounce of prevention" is worth far more than an attempt to "pound the cure into her." Prevention is the key to keeping your puppy both curious and safe as she explores her environment, so keep an eye on her while she plays.

The physical demands on your dog will come in spurts. A stroll around the block is just right for a little child. Your puppy will sit down and refuse to move if you take him or her on a stroll that is too lengthy. It's possible that you'll have to pick her up and bring her inside. Short, frequent walks are preferable to long, arduous ones.

Don't try to keep up with long distances of running with your dog. Limit the length of the runs. While it's acceptable to take your dog for a run on a long leash in a grassy area, you should wait until he or she is a year old before engaging in any high-impact activities like leaping or sprinting. You don't want to put a damper on their skeletal growth by injuring them while they're still maturing.

Your puppy's physical demands may be met with a very standard, but adequate, "recipe" of one or two short walks each day in addition to one or two brief runs. It's important to remember that various breeds need somewhat different changes to equilibrium.

Social Requirements

Right now, meeting your puppy's social requirements is crucial. Because she is still building her opinions and ideas about the world, this is one of her most pressing needs. Make sure your puppy meets plenty of new people, animals, and things by planning lots of outings for him or her now.

In terms of introducing your puppy to new people and environments, "the more the merrier" isn't necessarily the case. Never settle for less than the best. Limit your puppy's contact with other animals so it doesn't get frightened. Try going to new sites when they aren't as crowded. Introduce unfamiliar items with tasty treats. Your dog will pick up appropriate social behaviors at an accelerated rate with more pleasant encounters.

When anything (a loud noise or sudden movement) frightens a puppy, it might be tempting to pick it up and give it a "magic carpet ride," carrying it from one place to another and trying to comfort it as soon as possible. Puppies need to be allowed to fully experience new settings, but we must be conscious that there may be moments when scooping them up may avoid injury and a poor learning experience. Our pups will mimic our every action and conclude that something is amiss if they encounter anything unfamiliar.

Supply them with a "safety net." Help your puppy with things like stair climbing, car rides, and getting in and out of the vehicle. Since we don't want their itty-bitty furry joints to get hurt, we'll need to learn how much support to provide while still letting them adjust to their new home. Putting our hands under a child's armpits to "unweight" them as they start to walk is a good analogy for the kind of "safety net" we may provide for our pups in similar circumstances.

Most people don't realize how much sleep a puppy needs at this age. They can get their energy levels back up to puppy level by napping in a kennel in a quiet environment. A well-rested puppy is more likely to follow your lead, reduce his mouthing, work with you to master new skills, and enjoy time spent with you during play. The battery may be recharged by rest, but sleep is the most effective method. Your puppy is more likely to go into a deep slumber at night, when the lack of light makes it easier for him to relax.

Growth spurts increase the need to get enough sleep. The most rapid period of physical development occurs during the puppy years. During a growth spurt, your dog may lose interest in her usual activities and start sleeping almost all the time. As soon as the growth surge ends, she'll be right back to her old self.

Keep a close eye on your puppy at all times. If you keep a close eye on him and guide his every move, he will make fewer errors. The owner will feel less pressure if errors are reduced. Since the owner is under less pressure, he or she is less likely to have a tantrum or act like an "ugly owner." Puppy-human trust increases when leaders display less "stressed-out" behavior. Simple, right?

Limits Unknown: A puppy can't be corrected on something you don't know it doesn't know. Do not scold or verbally criticize your puppy if it ventures into unexplored territory, such as a room it is not allowed in. Call her by name and compliment her for following your example to win her over.

Keep your dog on a leash so that you may guide him in a less aversive direction. If you spot him getting into trouble, give the leash a little pull and speak his name calmly to grab his attention and get him out of trouble.

Remember that this is the time when the puppy really makes errors. Our pups could pick up the idea that exploring is bad if we react negatively to their missteps. At this point, errors are just that: mistakes. They need to know that their leaders will facilitate a peaceful and just education for them. Keep calm and refocus your puppy if he makes a mistake when housetraining, eating, or mouthing.

Have strong babysitting skills. Don't leave your puppy in the backyard or the living room to "play" by himself since we need to meet all of his requirements. Prepare some fun things to do with your dog while you're together. Your puppy may be kept active and entertained in a variety of constructive ways, such as with balls, chew toys, puppy manners exercises, walks, etc.

Put your dog in her kennel for a nap when you can't watch her. The simplest approach to avoiding mistakes It may be necessary to kennel her while you do things like pay bills or prepare supper. You may relax knowing that your puppy is secure in her cage whenever you can't keep an eye on her. Consider the alternatives to holding a kid, such as the walker, playpen, swing, and cot. Until the child is old enough to ride safely without assistance, tools, or "training wheels," are always utilized.

Make sure your dog has access to chew toys everywhere you take him. If you have some toys on hand, your dog will have something constructive to do while you put on your shoes or brush your teeth. That way, your legs, the table legs, and your leather shoes won't become the "chew toy du jour!"

Why Use a Crate for Dog Training?

The box is the most reliable and secure method of solitary confinement. Introduce it to your puppy as soon as possible and keep using it until it is fully grown (about two to three years). In many contexts, it ensures security and esteem. Crate training helps with housebreaking, boundary acceptance, puppy safety, property protection, and maintaining positive relationships.

Housebreaking: The crate is a great tool for housetraining your pet. Its purpose is to encourage neatness. Dogs naturally avoid soiling their own beds or dens.

Structure: Using the crate as a kind of structure is the simplest approach to teaching your dog to value obedience to authority figures. A puppy may learn to respect the household's norms by spending time in its box on a regular basis.

Recognizing Personal Limits: The cage creates acceptance of limits in your dog's life since it is a tangible barrier. One of your major aims with the puppy will be aided by this. Security of the Dog. You can't always be "tied" to your dog or watch her every move. Crate use is beneficial and appropriate in these scenarios as well. When you're not there to supervise it, any dog may get into trouble if it doesn't know the rules of the house. Puppy accidents at home include slipping down the stairs, chewing on cables, eating foreign objects, etc. When you need to step away from monitoring your puppy for a minute, she will be secure in her cage until you return.

Secured Premises: Nothing is more heartbreaking than coming home to find your brand-new dog has torn your $100 sneakers to shreds. It's also frustrating to be on the phone and see your baby using the DVD remote as a teething toy. These are normal puppy mishaps, despite common opinion, and may be avoided by cradling your puppy whenever he or she is alone.

Rescuer of Faltering Relationships: A healthy connection with your dog requires that you both get some space from time to time. We and our pups are equally at risk of behaving badly when we are overtired and stressed. When we're anxious, our voices and body language change, and our pups may learn damaging behaviors. Our connection may be jeopardized by the loss of either patience or something of value. A relationship saver, the crate provides a solution to the age-old query, "How can I miss you if you don't go away?"

Dog toys that exercise the dog's mind and alleviate boredom

The old adage goes something like, "A dog that's tired is a good dog." But what exactly does it imply? Should you regularly exercise your dog by taking him on long runs or hikes? Should you wear out your dog by playing tug or fetch with him? While it's true that many canines may benefit from more physical activity, remember that keeping your dog's mind active and engaged is just as crucial if you want him to calm down and behave like a family member. What does it mean to have one's mind stimulated? Do you remember how fatigued you used to get after sitting at a desk for 7 hours a day? Even though you hadn't run very far, you were exhausted. That's because your mind was spent after a day of learning and digesting new information.

Perhaps you were solving complex equations, debating philosophical ideas, analyzing works of literature, and having deep, thought-provoking conversations. Just like the muscles in your body, your brain needs fuel (in the form of food, vitamins, and minerals) in order to work properly. In addition to giving our dogs lots of physical activity, it is crucial that we help them utilize their minds so that they feel intellectually exhausted. What does it imply for our canine companions? Have you ever returned after a 6-mile walk to find your dog eager to play after just 20 minutes of rest?

If this sounds like your dog, it's time to start looking at methods to get their brain working as hard as their body. The significance of both physical activity and mental stimulation and training cannot be overstated. Although many of our canine friends would benefit from more physical exercise, it is also important to vary your dog's routine and provide mental stimulation to ensure that your dog is both physically and psychologically exhausted. Increasing your dog's physical activity may have the unintended consequence of making them more fit for future workouts rather than wearing them out. There are several options for enriching your dog's mental life. Talk to other pet owners you know, do some research online, and use your imagination to come up with even more methods to keep your dog's mind active and engaged than the ones on this list.

Training Courses, Both Beginner and Advanced: It seems logical that this would be the starting point. Please enroll your dog in a training class immediately if you haven't already done so. Having a good time as you train your dog Training your dog has several benefits, including strengthening your relationship with him or her and making him more obedient to your commands. This has the dual benefit of creating a psychologically exhausted dog that is eager to interact with you. Always remember to put everything you've learned into practice at home, on walks, and everywhere else you and your dog go!

"Puzzle Toys," "Treat Dispensing Toys," or "Work-to-Eat" Toys: Provide your dog's food in a toy that requires him to think and maneuver in order to get the kibble out, as opposed to a dish full of kibble that will be devoured in under a minute. You may now get a wide selection of toys designed to provide mental stimulation for your dog while he eats. A Kong filled with a combination of dry kibble and canned food is one alternative, as are the following toys designed specifically for dry kibble: The IQ Treat Ball, the Buster Food Cube, the Kong Wobbler, the Buster Food Cube, the Buster Kibble Nibble, the Buster Magic Mushroom, and the Buster Food Cube You may also get a wide selection of slow-feeding dog bowls and puzzle toys for extended mealtimes from businesses like Outward Hound and Ethical Pet. Because he needs to think about how to get his food, your dog will be more psychologically exhausted after a mealtime that requires him to work for it.

Third, play games with your dog that require him to use his nose to keep his mind sharp. Say the command, "Find it!" and throw the treat on the floor to teach your dog the command. You'll know your dog knows "Find it!" when he or she begins looking for the food on the floor BEFORE you've thrown it. Put a treat or a couple of pieces of kibble in a cardboard box or other similar container, and tell your dog, "Find it!" after he or she knows the game. Start by making the search area small so your dog can quickly find his or her way around. Then, explore new avenues of thought. Hide old cereal or pasta boxes behind chairs, the dining table, or behind furniture, and lure your dog out with goodies hidden under the boxes.

Instruct Tricks There are several publications that detail the steps necessary to train your dog to perform tricks like shake paws, spin, leap through hoops, pick up his toys, etc. Carefully seek out a book that uses rewards-based training to ensure that you are rewarding your dog with pleasant experiences as he learns new skills. Teaching your dog tricks is a fun way to wear out your dog's mind and a great method to strengthen your bond with your dog via reinforcement-based training.

Incorporate training into playtime. Think back to when you took your dog to obedience school. Use them on occasion and reinforce them with your dog's favorite items. Does your dog like games of fetch, for instance? Get him to sit still and hold that pose before you toss the ball. Is your dog also a fan of the game of tug? Make him wait until he is seated before telling him to "take it!" Whatever you command your dog to perform in preparation for the ball's release is irrelevant. To prevent your dog from being too rambunctious during playtime, this might also teach him to relax and concentrate when playing.

Having a good time with food

This is a great game to play when you don't have much time but still want to stimulate your dog's mind. Why not make your dog earn his food instead of just giving it to him in a dish? You earned that money, after all! It simply takes a few seconds to devour a platter of food. Scattered treats in the yard or around the house may take your dog several minutes to track down and devour, keeping him occupied in a constructive manner while also stimulating areas of his brain that wouldn't get much use otherwise.

Confused thoughts

Spread your dog's food out over a short space, ideally on a flat surface where he can see it easily. When your dog has mastered this, you may go on to toss it over a larger area or onto grass to challenge his sense of smell as well as his sight. If your dog is very adept at locating his food, you might increase the difficulty by hiding it in thicker grass or behind shrubs. A "food trail" may be created by scattering the food items in a long, haphazard line. This is such a fun game for my dogs that they become quite depressed when I serve them their food in a dish instead. Though wet food isn't the best option for scatter feeding, you can still make it work by dividing your dog's daily serving up among many smaller containers and concealing them throughout the home and yard. Your dog will have a great time searching for food and eating it in little increments. You may also give your dog wet food that you place inside a Kong and let him chew and lick to release it. Put your dog's meal inside the Kong and put it in the freezer for a cool puzzle to play with on hot days. Enjoy this in the fresh air!

A bottled message

First, choose a plastic water bottle that is empty and of an appropriate size. Make sure it's the kind that crumples when you compress it instead of tearing. Dogs vary greatly in their persistence; some may quit if they don't see results right away, while others will attempt to gnaw their way to the rewards. You may lend a hand by placing 'easy wins' in the bottle's spout so they spill out without any effort on anyone's part. Safety First Keep a close eye on your dog if he decides to use the treat bottle as a toy. Replace the bottle often and inspect it for damage.

Second, take off the bottle's label and plastic ring from its neck.

Third, to pique your dog's curiosity, fill the bottle with his dry food and shake it. Include some really pungent morsels at the start, such as little chunks of cheese or hotdog sausage, so he gets a taste of the deliciousness to come.

Give the bottle to your dog and let him figure out how to open it to obtain the goodies inside. Others will shake it, others will roll it, and some will toss it.

That quickly!

There are several advantages to stimulating your dog's mental abilities. The first is that he is far less likely to seek out riddles to solve on his own, such as how to empty the kitchen bin or escape from the garden, if you are occupied with him solving puzzles that you have developed. The second benefit is that it may assist in channeling energy that would otherwise need to be burned off by giving your dog physical exercise since solving problems requires cerebral work. Twenty minutes of fun mental stimulation for your dog is worth an hour of physical activity, and both of you will be satisfied with the results. This is helpful for both high-energy puppies and older dogs whose physical activity is limited, maybe due to health issues. It's also helpful in teaching dogs with behavioral issues the basics of mindfulness and concentration.

Digging Inside

A lot of dogs need a place to dig. It's not simply a matter of preference; it's a matter of need. Some dog breeds, like Dachshunds, have the instinct to dig 'hard-wired' into their brains since they were developed specifically for the purpose of tracking underground prey. It's possible that digging is merely a "phase" for some breeds, especially while they're young or growing up. It's possible that these dogs are just having fun making a golf course out of your yard and are in need of a healthy distraction. Throw some goodies inside the box, so your dog needs to bend in to receive them if he is hesitant to put his front paws in.

Refrain from picking him up and bringing him in; doing so might further set him off and squander a chance to help him help himself. Select a box with shallow sides and positively reinforce your dog's entry and exit to build his self-assurance. Honor his effort by clicking the link below. Add a few more goodies to the box, but this time cover them with an old towel, some crumpled-up paper, or a piece of cardboard that is around the same size as the floor of the box. Doggy treats are more fun when they require some digging.

Indoor Games of Hide and Seek

Dogs have a natural curiosity and like exploring new areas in search of treats and playthings. Playing hide-and-seek inside may be a fun mental challenge for your dog and a good alternative to taking him outside when it's raining. The act of making your dog wait while you go for the toy or treat teaches him patience and may help him perfect his "wait" or "stay" manners. If you have a new puppy or a dog that has just been adopted, it may be better to start with food concealed within a container than with the dog's favorite toy.

Basics

Roll up the end of a toilet paper tube and stuff it with some tasty, odoriferous delights. Put the top down. Introduce your dog to the tube by allowing him to smell it. If your dog knows how to wait or remain, have him do so while you sneak the tube out of sight. It is cheating if he even moves one inch. After you've tucked the tube away, come back to your dog and give him the "release" command. To the extent that he needs encouragement, give it to him on his own terms. Your dog should be encouraged to retrieve the tube as soon as he discovers it.

What's trendy and what's not in chewing

Dogs may be easily entertained by playing with a toy that contains their favorite treat. All chew toys are not created equal, however. Dogs don't give a lick about many things that humans find appealing, while other things that we wouldn't give a second look to are doggie paradise. So, what's trendy and what's not in your dog's book?

136

For most dogs, nothing compares to a Kong when it comes to a satisfying chewing experience. Select the appropriate size and strength (black is the strongest) to match your dog's jaw strength and perseverance. The nicest part of the Kong is that it can be loaded with treats to provide entertainment for minutes or even hours. It takes skill to fill a Kong, so here are a few ideas: Cheese-based treats Use the back of a teaspoon to press some cheese into the very bottom of the Kong. Spread on some peanut butter or marmite for more flavor. Freeze pops for dogs Wrap cling film around the outside of the Kong's bottom. Put some wet dog food in the Kong or some chunks of meat floating in some kind of sauce. Put it in the freezer in a safe manner.

Ideally enjoyed on warm summer nights (but only in the garden!), Additional faceted Nyla bones are another great chewing option. Nylon toys are scented to make them more appealing to aggressive chewers; they are safe for all but the tiniest of teeth, but you should still change them often to avoid injuries. Fish skin chews, however, are both delicious and harmless. They are digestible and available in a variety of forms, including rolls and twists, making them ideal for dogs with digestive issues.

Think Seriously About What You Want and Can Offer a dog.

After making the decision to have a dog, the next step is to figure out what breed is ideal for you. If you know what you want in a dog and what you can provide for it, choosing the perfect breed will be a breeze. And so will the fortunate canine who gets to go home with you. It's not as easy as choosing the prettiest puppy you see, no matter how much you want to do so.

The so-called wolfdog was the primary topic of discussion in an episode of the Dog Whisperer reality show on National Geographic. Wolf-dog hybrids are known as wolfdogs. Some people are curious when they see an ad for a wolf puppy because wolves have captivated humans for hundreds of years. They desire to be landowners. Wolfdogs are adorable, especially as puppies. But as time goes on, the owner realizes that this is no ordinary dog; wolves are predators, and the dog will do everything it takes to defend what it believes to be its territory. When a wolfdog acts in accordance with its nature, its owner may misinterpret the behavior as bad manners. The wolfdog is quickly confined in a cage or sent to a shelter, where it is euthanized.

Cooperates with Other Dogs in Playgroup Recalls

It won't take long for your dog to associate the command "come" with the reward of coming to you immediately. Having her practice coming while she's interacting with other dogs is the next stage. Test it out with the canine companions of your friends and neighbors. See the sidebar "Recall Games with Friends and Family" (below) for several enjoyable methods to practice with others that will help improve recalls dramatically, and try practicing in less demanding locations or with fewer other dogs if you're having problems.

Get your dog's focus on the reward and call her to you while you're among a group of dogs. Don't be reticent. If necessary, place the reward directly on the dog's nose to encourage him to follow you. Don't pay attention to the other dogs, even if they're eyeing your goodie. Keep your attention on your dog to keep her attention on you. "Watch" Test how long you can maintain your dog's focus by gradually increasing the distance between you. You may use the term "come" as many times as you want to get her attention. At this point, it is OK to repeat the term since it is still an "exercise" and not a "command." Keep moving until she is bored, then invite her to sit and watch.

Here are some entertaining methods to work on your recalls with the aid of your loved ones. The exercise "Back-and-Forth Recalls" (number 59) is one example: The dog won't know who is going to call her next if you and your friends stand in a circle and take turns calling her at irregular intervals. When playing any of these activities with your dog, it is important that you reward him or her whenever he or she returns to you. If you and a friend are all alone, you may take turns calling the dog.

However, after she recognizes the routine, she may begin circling the area without stopping to reply, "Come." If your dog ever returns to you when you haven't called her, the person she's trying to avoid should call her back and lavish her with praise until she comes back. As a result, students learn that the command to "come" means to stop what they're doing and go back to the person who called them. In addition, do this anytime your dog interacts with other canine playmates. You may summon your dog through the pack if you stand on the borders and walk him or her back and forth. The association between "come" and "pay no attention to anything else and come back to me" is strengthened in this way.

The traditional recall game played in a circle may be modified in several ways. After the initial setup of the game, you should begin spreading out. When someone else in the group calls your dog, you should all take a step back or change locations. The first little circle will quickly expand into a much larger one. Then the enjoyable game of hide-and-seek may begin, with individuals ducking behind furniture and around corners. Try out some of these moves and come up with some of your own. Recall drills with them are enjoyable and simple.

Changes To Elegant Endings

Combining recalls with creative endings is another enjoyable method to practice working with recalls (see exercise 25). This practice isn't required, but it's worth your time because of the "cool" effect, much like fancy finishes themselves. However, you should wait to undertake this exercise until your dog has a good stay command (see Part 5), since doing so before then might weaken your stay command. The "Session Plan" section at the back of the book provides extra information on how to best organize the introduction of these activities.

Down-Stay

Expect your dog to mess up the remain command at first, and keep in mind that failure is a crucial part of learning. Before your dog fails at the stay and is "corrected," it is not really learning the stay. She's simply chilling out as we feed her. Only by pointing out and fixing her blunders can you get the results you need from her. In other words, do not get frustrated since correction is a necessary part of the process. Learn to use a "negative marker" to express displeasure and improve your communication skills. It's important to make the process as simple as possible for your dog. Feast on the success of even the smallest steps forward. Take it gradually and steadily expand your routines rather than trying to accomplish too much too soon and failing every time, and you'll see the results far more quickly. Your dog's and your own self-assurance will suffer as a result of this.

Leaving Behind a Down-and-Out Situation

Your dog will learn the meaning of "stay" after a few rounds of correction. If so, the next logical move is to get up and walk away from her. It's crucial that you NOT hold a treat in the hand you use to indicate. This holds true whether you're staying in a seated, standing, or lying posture. When you hold a treat in your signal hand, your dog may mistakenly believe you are trying to lure her towards you. After all, rewards are used in the same way for any other kind of physical activity. Instead, as you walk away, hide the treat in the palm of your opposite hand, then swiftly reveal it and praise her. You should execute this "moving away" exercise many times and then either give your dog a release command (such as "take a break") or go on to something else. In the beginning, however, you should NOT practice recalls while the dog is still.

How To Get Inspired by The Ball: Fundamentals

Your dog may be favorably motivated in a variety of ways. So far, we've been using treats, which is the simplest and most commonly applicable option. However, goodies aren't your only option. Some dogs respond equally well, if not better, to balls and other toys than they do to rewards. Furthermore, if rewards are used too often, they may be used for surface-level rather than

145

foundational training. Adding a strong relationship component to an otherwise transactional training program through the use of balls as motivators and games as incentives might help correct this imbalance. Part 6 demonstrates how to include balls in some of the exercises shown in parts 1 through 5. Meanwhile, supplementary exercises shown on my website at www.doggonegood.org/book-bonus expand upon these methods, demonstrating how to utilize balls in more difficult settings and for more difficult instructions. If your dog enjoys playing with balls, toys, and games, you may utilize them to your advantage in training.

Some dog trainers persist in believing that dogs learn dominating and maybe violent behaviors by playing tug-of-war. Or, you may have heard that if you don't win every game of tug-of-war, your dog won't respect you as the "alpha." That's ridiculous! At least one investigation into whether or not playing tug-of-war is linked to aggressive or domineering tendencies turned up nothing. If you and your dog follow these guidelines, tug-of-war may be one of the most enjoyable activities you can do together. Set the rules, take charge, and call it a day. Put simply. So, what does this entail? When you're ready to play, "initiate the game" by bringing out the toys. Don't give in when your dog comes over with the old rope toy, thrusts it into your crotch, and begs for a game.

Every thirty seconds or so, "control the game" means to order off (see part 10) and then ask your dog for any command. You may "end the game" by telling your dog, "That's enough," or by putting away the toy. Finally, it's okay to give your dog the occasional victory. After all, why bother with a lose-lose game? If you're hoping to raise a dominant dog, this won't do it. Dominant canines often give up access to valuable resources to their subordinates because they know they can easily reclaim them with a simple stroll over and a "woof." If you want the toy back, just go up to your dog, give the order "off," and the dog should gladly give it back to you. If you have taught your dog well, she will pay attention to you, follow your instructions, and look forward to the next round. This is all helpful for training's social aspect.

Retrieving a lost ball by hitting it with another ball

If you use a ball to motivate your dog, she may be hesitant to return without the ball. She may instead provoke you into a game of "keep-away" by attempting to have you grasp at the ball. Don't do that, and don't tell her to pass by saying "off." Because of this, her cheerful outlook will be shattered, and she may lose interest in the ball altogether. Here's an easy way to get around it: Get your dog's attention with one of two similar balls. Hurl it. When she comes back and still won't give it up, get out the second ball and play with her. Keep your hands on it! At least, not until the ball in her mouth becomes boring and she drops it in favor of the one you're holding. Then, without letting her see it, toss the ball across her line of vision. Keep up with her as she races to catch the tossed ball, picking up the one she drops so you may start again when she returns.

Your dog will rapidly spit out the ball in her mouth after playing this game ten to twenty times to get you to throw the one in your hand. It's a done deal. Alternatively, you may try rewarding her with a treat whenever she returns the ball instead of giving her a new one. This, however, is not as efficient or sleek. Even when offered a reward, some dogs may continue to play "keep-away." Injecting a reward may disrupt the flow of training, divert your dog's attention, and run counter to your efforts to reduce the number of goodies used. In any case, give it a try and see if this is the one that helps your dog the most.

Some dogs have trouble letting go of the ball once they get it because they are torn between two drives: the prey drive and the play drive. This is the catch: Once you have a hold of your prey, you shouldn't let it go, since this is a cardinal rule of prey drive. Why? Taking in food is a primordial and essential need, and so is avoiding becoming prey. Therefore, a dog has a hardwired insistence on hold as to the prey item at all costs. The goal of play drive, on the other hand, is to maintain the continuity of play. That's all there is to it. Even though dogs are not dimwitted and know that the tennis ball is not a prey item, their prey drive instructs them to "never let go." Typically, dogs will change the fetch game into a game of keep-away in order to balance these competing instincts. By doing so, the dog is able to retain the prey item and play the game again. By switching to the two-ball routine, you may avoid this problem by providing your dog with a second prey item to chase.

Chapter 5

Pick Up Some Dog language

Dogs are great communicators, if only humans could decipher them. Behaviors like backing away, cowering, or tucking the tail between the legs are indicators of fear. If they move their head away, cover their jaws, or flip their ears back, it's because they're uncomfortable. If you ignore these warnings, a dog may become aggressive. Dogs' "good" wags are moderate in height, relatively slow, and accompanied by a calm demeanor. However, dogs may also wave "hi!" from afar by wagging their tails high when anxious or low when calm. According to the available research, young children have a hard time reading the body language of dogs, making it difficult for them to discern symptoms of anxiety or tension in dogs. It is the responsibility of the adults present to keep a careful eye on the youngster and the dog and to end the activity if either one seems to be struggling.

We have effectively molded the natural behavior of dogs since they were first domesticated and educated to be our pets and friends so that they may share our lives, homes, and environments. However, there are several instincts that can't be bred or trained out of a dog: When threatened, many dogs will aggressively defend their territory, with some even resorting to biting or attacking. Moreover, although many people associate certain breeds with aggression, any dog is capable of attacking a human.

Keep Calm and Carry On If A Dog Attacks you.

The most essential thing to remember if an angry dog is racing at you is to remain calm and not make any sudden movements or noises. Keep your cool and don't make direct eye contact with anybody.

Leave their presence as calmly and gradually as you can. Right, Yourself If a dog is charging at you, stand tall, don't move, and dial 911. If you have the luxury of time, try putting an object (a clipboard, a jacket, a trash can) between you and the dog. If you find yourself on the floor, roll into the smallest ball possible. Most canines have excellent "bite inhibition." If a dog is afraid and you approach it without realizing it, it may bite once to warn you off, but it probably won't keep biting if you get away. IF ANOTHER PERSON IS UNDER ASSAULT, TAKE PRECAUTIONS. Know that you run the risk of being bitten if you try to break up a fight between two dangerous people. Put the dog off guard. You may accomplish this by calling out from a distance, using your automobile horn, or using a hose to spray the animal if one is available and it is safe to do so.

Dogs shouldn't be reprimanded for the occasional snarl. Growling is a very dangerous signal, particularly around youngsters, and has to be managed and trained immediately. However, this is straightforward canine communication. Your pet may stop growling if you punish him or her, but his or her underlying discomfort (or fear) will remain. This implies that a dog may not show any signs of aggression before biting. If you laugh off signals of anxiety or tension, you might end up hurting yourself and others. Interactions that are causing problems should be stopped immediately, and a professional dog trainer should be consulted if necessary. Keep in mind that a dog requires privacy when resting or eating. Children should never enter a dog's personal space. Children also need time alone, away from the dogs (maybe in their bedroom), or in a "safe" environment.

Keep your distance from any dogs you may encounter. A dog's outside status does not always imply that it welcomes attention from strangers. Even if a dog enjoys going on walks with kids, that doesn't mean it's necessarily friendly to other people's kids. Wait until the dog is not tied up in front of a store (or you can't locate their parent) before introducing yourself. Animal owners should never feel obligated to have their dog say "hi!" to stranger children, but should instead pay attention to the dog's cues and give the animal the freedom to decline any pats from stranger children. Skipping this one encounter is not going to injure anything, and it will teach youngsters valuable lessons about giving animals their space.

Speech is the primary non-written mode of human interaction. This is not the case with the dog. The dog mostly uses body language to convey its messages. Consider the good and bad effects our bodies may have on our pets.

Your dogs can read your intentions from the expression on your face, the way you stand and walk, the direction from which you approach them, the way you carry yourself, and the way you "reach" for them.

It's important to tailor your strategy to each individual dog. Some dogs need you to project an image of authority. You can adopt an attitude that makes you seem taller. A relaxed body posture and a neutral approach (not head-on) might help certain dogs regard you as more friendly and accessible.

Statements such as "Come play!" and "I'm pleased with your behavior!" "I'm proud of you!", and "I'm your leader, and you can trust me" are examples of positive messages. There is a certain set of body language signals that must be used to express each message.

It is common knowledge that a slouched posture, open arms, and a sitting stance are all indicators of friendly body language. The pace at which you walk might express either warmth or fervor.

If you want to approach an anxious or shy dog, you should do it from the side. When playing on the sidelines, you should take a neutral," or defensive, stance. Don't try to "sneak attack" me from behind, however. Take it easy and go at a modest pace.

When trying to convey authority, a "softer" body position (i.e., rounded shoulders) is less effective than a square or erect one. Maintain a confident, upright posture while giving orders. This stance will give off an authoritative but not aggressive vibe.

Intimidation, threats, and forceful leadership are all examples of the kinds of negative signals to avoid. These are the ones that warn, "You're really in trouble now, buster!" These forms of body language have no place in "civilized" human-canine dialogue. For dogs to have a chance of survival in the wild, they need access to resources like these.

Does a dog's need to chew provide cerebral stimulation?

Absolutely! Toys for dogs are wonderful for their mental health since chewing is a meditative and focused activity. A long-lasting dog toy may be used for solo playtime or to foster interaction between canine companions.

Your dog's intelligence will be put to good use as it concentrates on biting all the varied angles and edges of this unconventionally formed chew toy.

How much stimulation do dogs need in terms of mental stimulation?

You should give your dog at least 30 minutes of playtime every day, preferably in two 15-minute intervals throughout the day. Dogs have different mental stimulation requirements, so it's crucial to keep an eye on your pet and tailor his or her playtime accordingly. Large, hyperactive breeds need more mental stimulation than smaller, calmer ones.

What are some effective brain exercises for dogs?

The good news is that there is no shortage of ways to engage a dog's mind. You can simply include many of these brain games for dogs into your dog's everyday routine to help improve their focus and behavior.

Hide-and-Seek

Playing mental games with your dog, such as Hide and Seek, might help develop his or her problem-solving abilities. Dog commands like "wait" and "come," as well as novel ones like "find," may be practiced and expanded upon during this outing.

You may test your dog's ability to "find" you by hiding goodies, toys, or even yourself in a variety of games.

Dog Parlor Games

Canine Mastering the 'Paw' Trick Involving your dog in the process of learning a new skill is like giving their brain a rigorous workout! Your dog's self-esteem and happiness may benefit from your training methods if you use positive reinforcement to teach it new skills. Don't forget to show plenty of excitement and appreciation.

Though 'paw' and 'shake hands' are among the most well-known dog tricks, there are really hundreds more that you can teach your pet. Some entertaining ploys that are also excellent mental games include:

- Relax and lay back.
- Put the door shut.
- Remain Calm and Cross Your legs.

Dispersed feeding

Scatter feeding is the practice of dispersing food and rewards across the home or yard in order to stimulate a dog's foraging instincts. All you have to do to start this form of enrichment exercise is let your dog seek out and smell out its food across a designated area.

Dogs have an acute sense of smell, so nose training activities like scatter feeding may be a fun way to exercise that sense while also teaching independence from the traditional feeding bowl.

Puzzles Involving Food

Keeping with the theme of feeding, food puzzles are another popular kind of dog brain game since they require your dog to exert mental effort in exchange for a tasty reward. You may either purchase a food puzzle for your dog online or construct one yourself at home.

Memory and problem-solving abilities are enhanced, while tension is reduced and digestion is enhanced, when a dog plays with these puzzles. A dog's eating pace will slow while using a puzzle feeder since it takes more time to figure out how to move the puzzle pieces so that the dog can get to all of the food in each hole.

Engaging Canine Playthings, Number Five

Toys for dogs may be utilized in a variety of mental exercises. Toys exist in a wide variety of forms and functions, each of which contributes to the delight and variety of play.

Dogs' mental faculties benefit from playing with squeaky toys since they attract their attention and satisfy their need to chew and play. Toys for dogs that roll or bounce in all directions provide mental challenges as well. The Dog Is Being Taught to Drop it.

Store Toys When Done playing.

Dogs who know the 'drop it' or 'give it' command might benefit from learning to place their toys back in the toy box, basket, or container after playing is over.

A dog's innate desire to fetch and retrieve is catered to by this mental challenge. Not only does this help you and your dog wind down and communicate the end of fun, but it also gives them some freedom and relieves you of a potential cleaning chore.

Relay Races with Obstacles

Making your dog run through an obstacle course has numerous positive effects. They are beneficial for training the intellect, but they also aid in physical fitness and quickness.

You may enroll your dog in agility training courses in your region, or you can use commonplace items like chairs, bed sheets, mops, and brooms to create a fun obstacle course in your home or yard. Your dog will have a great time working off some steam as it navigates its way through the various obstacles.

Indulge Your Dog's Natural Curiosity on walks.

Your dog's day will be made if he or she gets to go for a stroll. Allowing them to pause and sniff around will provide them with more mental stimulation. Dogs benefit physically from walks, but the experience is multifaceted for them. Even if you've gone down the same street a thousand times, that doesn't mean there aren't interesting scents for your dog to investigate every time.

Make your dog earn their meals.

When it comes to mealtime, it's quite straightforward for our dogs. Usually, we simply leave their dish on the floor and walk away while they eat. There's certainly nothing wrong with it, but it's a big departure from the way most of them normally behave. So, if you want to give your dog some extra brain exercise, try switching up his or her meal schedule. Make feeding time an exciting game for your dog instead of simply passing them their food a couple times a day.

Invest in a Brain Teaser for Fido.

When it comes to keeping your dog amused and occupied, puzzle toys are a great choice. Toys that require your dog to utilize his brain, like puzzles, might help him stay focused on his work for longer. Adding only 15 minutes of playtime every day may make a tremendous impact on your dog. It offers them purpose in their day, which is a key factor in reducing problematic behavior. Dogs benefit greatly from puzzle toys because they allow their innate intelligence to be put to work. And by playing with them, you may enhance your dog's self-assurance and wear out its brain.

Try Out Some no-cost molding games.

In shaping, your dog is rewarded whenever he or she displays the desired behavior throughout training. It's a lot of fun for you and your dog, and it's a terrific opportunity to teach him some new skills or behaviors. Select the behavior you want to modify as the starting point. Anything from sitting down to putting their nose on your hand is OK. When your dog exhibits the desired behavior, make sure to click or say "yes" to reinforce the behavior. Because you want to encourage the behavior you desire, click or say "yes" as soon as your dog delivers the behavior. Your dog will rapidly pick up on the behaviors you want and start providing them more regularly if you are patient and consistent with your rewards. Mentally challenging your dog with fun activities is a terrific way to bond with him or her. Why not attempt shaping as a fun and simple entry point?

Engage Your Dog in a Game of "Shells"

The shell game is a great technique to provide cerebral stimulation for your dog. Your dog will enjoy playing this game, and it will also help them develop critical thinking abilities. You and your dog will need three individual cups and a modest reward in order to play the shell game. Toss the cups about and hide the reward in one of them. Give your dog some time to explore and pick out a cup on his own. They only earn the reward if they choose the right cup. You may increase the difficulty of this game by using a larger number of cups and switching up where you hide the reward each time you play with your dog.

Now, bear in mind that not all dogs are equally enthusiastic about puzzle toys. My dog would rather play with a frozen Kong filled with food than a flat puzzle toy. A jigsaw toy could keep her occupied for 2 minutes, but a frozen Kong will keep her entertained for 30 or more. Make a puzzle using a muffin pan and some tennis balls to see whether your dog likes them.

You can train your dog to do new tricks

Can your dog do any tricks? I hope they have a nice time here and get some rest. However, there is a wealth of information beyond the fundamentals that you may impart to them. One can never learn enough tricks.

Teaching your dog, a new trick or command is great for mental stimulation, and it can be especially helpful with shy or fearful dogs. All that training will help boost your dog's confidence, and it will strengthen the bond between dog and owner. Learning new commands can also help increase your dog's focus and impulse control.

Being a responsible pet owner requires a holistic approach to their health and wellbeing. Training and exercise are major contributors to your dog's health and wellbeing. Their time with you is likely their favorite part of the day, so whether it's spent physically exercising together, playing outside, or learning new tricks, this time together strengthens your bond.

How much exercise does my dog need? How far do I take my dog's training? Can my dog entertain themselves? Each dog is an individual, so finding the right mental and physical exercise for them will need to be tailored to suit. Finding activities to suit their personalities and activity levels is a fun exercise. We've got a few suggestions for mental and physical exercise to help you on your quest.

Ongoing training with your dog can be so fun and rewarding for both of you. Training is mentally stimulating for your dog, and it strengthens the bond you have.

If you're lucky enough to be at the puppy stage in your pet parent journey, you will find puppy pre-schools aplenty, as they are usually operated by dog trainers, vet clinics, and pet stores. This is a great program for socialization and basic training. The benefit of going through puppy preschool with a trainer is that you can usually move on to obedience training with them, and most trainers will come to your home to do some one-on-one training if you require it.

Depending on your dog's requirements, you may work with a training school to do ongoing training. Once you know your dog's strengths and interests, you may develop this routine into a more specialized activity like agility or flyball.

If scheduled classes aren't for you and you're self-motivated, you can check out some training videos at poochesatplay.com or YouTube to learn some tricks at home. Everybody loves meeting a dog that can shake or 'high five'.

Games

Not all dogs require the mental stimulation of extended training programs, and we understand that this won't fit every lifestyle, but there are other ways to exercise your dog's brain.

Dogs love to sniff! Setting up foraging hunts in the yard with some treats is an excellent activity for dogs. You will also find that there are lots of puzzles and enrichment toys available for pets; you just need to pop in some treats for your dog to sniff out.

Bones

Another activity that calls on their natural instincts is bending bones. A raw, meaty bone can be swapped out for a meal to not only help clean your dog's teeth but also provide them with mental stimulation. The challenge of ripping meat off a bone and having a bit of a gnaw might seem pretty gross for us humans, but for most dogs, this is living'. If you're not sure which bones are suitable for your dog, we have a handy guide to bones to help.

Exercise

Exercising your puppy

While your puppy is very young, their exercise is usually in the form of short bursts of play around the house or yard as well as their training. Don't underestimate how exhausting metal exercise can be, and it's an important part of your ongoing stimulation for your dog.

It's important not to encourage long, repetitive exercise sessions (like a jog with you, for example) for your puppy as they are growing. Depending on their breed, their joint plates won't fully fuse until

12–24 months, and this needs to happen before your dog can join you on a run. This will help prevent skeletal problems like hip dysplasia and arthritis in their older years.

Exercising adult dogs

Adult dogs require around 30–60 minutes of exercise each day. For some active breeds, they will need aerobic exercise daily, which may be for 30 minutes or more. Exercise isn't just important for health; it can also help with your dog's behavior. As the saying goes, 'a tired dog is a good dog, and a balanced combination of physical and mental exercise will mean you have a good and happy dog.

When it comes to physical exercise, always check the conditions outside, and be sure to bring some water and a collapsible bowl on hot days for water intervals. Avoid walking on the road or footpath when it's hot, as your dog's paws are sensitive and can easily burn on a hot road. A good rule of thumb is that if it's too hot for you to comfortably place the back of your hand on the pavement for a long period of time, then it's too hot for your dog's feet.

A tired dog is a happy dog.

There are many ways to exercise and stimulate your dog, and it depends on your dog's individual needs and your lifestyle to determine how you'll do this. After 20 years in the industry, we can say that a dog who is happily exercised and isn't bored is much less likely to be destructive or frustrated, which makes for a much happier and peaceful life with your dog.

Why Is Mental Exercise Important for Dogs?

Let's put it this way: A mentally stimulated dog is a happy dog. While it's important to make sure your dog gets enough physical activity each day, it's equally important that they get enough mental exercise too. Believe it or not, mental fatigue can make your dog more tired than physical fatigue. That's why mental exercise decreases hyperactivity, boredom, and destructive behaviors.

One day, give your dog rigorous physical activity, like an extra-long play session or a hike. Another day, give them a mental game to play (we'll have plenty of examples later in this article) and see which day they seem more tired.

- In a nutshell, mental exercise provides your dog with an outlet for excess energy while also keeping them out of mischief. Which leads us to the following subject:

- If your canine companions could talk, you'd likely hear them say, "I'm bored." They can't, however. Instead, kids act badly, destroy furniture, and make you crazy. Dogs must have mental exercise to prevent this. Keeping your dog's mind busy is an essential part of maintaining their contentment, calmness, and relaxation. When Fido is happy, so are Mommy and Daddy. In keeping with the theme of youth, we also have a number of excellent brain teaser games for your canine companion. You are thus in a perfect setting for stimulating your dog's intelligence!

- Your dog will greatly benefit from the mental challenge of nose work. It's a simple and enjoyable game that you can play with your pet, and it's a wonderful way to strengthen your relationship with each other. It's also an excellent method of wearing them down.

- You and your dog may have a lot of fun together engaging in various forms of nose work activities. Hiding puppy goodies around the house and challenging your dog to discover them is a fun activity. The two of you will have a blast while satisfying their innate need to search for hidden treasure.

- Making a smell trail and having your dog follow it is another fun way to practice nose skills. Fabric may be scented by rubbing an aromatic substance, such as orange peel, into it. The next step is to give your dog the cloth once it has been hidden. This is a fun and effective way to train your dog to follow their nose.

- Nose work is a great way to mentally stimulate your dog and bond with them at the same time. So, get out there and start playing some nose-work games with your furry friend today!

Conclusion

If you're looking for fun games for dogs that work as great brain training techniques for your dog, the above-mentioned steps are an excellent way to do so. Exercises are not only fun for your dog, but they can also help improve their mental well-being. There are a variety of different brain-training games and activities that you can do with your dog, so be sure to find one that suits their personality and needs. With a little patience, effort, and yummy Dog See training treats, you'll be able to see a noticeable difference in your dog's behavior in no time.

Our very own pets, several of which have traveled beside us over the course of the years, have left an indelible mark on our hearts, and a connection to them will remain with us forever. The cherished creatures that are currently a part of our lives and who have committed themselves to becoming our friends They've been quite patient with us while we worked on this paper, waiting and watching the whole time. They would sometimes provide a much-needed respite from writing, and other times they would just "lean" on her or gently kiss her to express their admiration and support.

Because you have a basis in the obedience lifestyle, having a good time with your excellent dog is all about engaging in enjoyable activities and making the most of the opportunities that these activities provide. One of the most crucial lessons we've learned as seasoned dog trainers is that a wide range of factors can influence behaviors. We think that rather than seeing the process of training your dog as a method to "fix" him or her, you should think of it as a journey towards creating a bond and a relationship that will last a lifetime with your pet. Good training is not just for dogs who cause problems.

Made in United States
Troutdale, OR
05/04/2024

19644081R00100